Developing GREEN

Strategies for Success

by Jerry Yudelson, PE, MBA, LEED AP

naiop
National Association of
Industrial and Office Properties

The Forum for Commercial Real Estate

Library of Congress Cataloging-in-Publication Data

Yudelson, Jerry.
  Developing green : strategies for success / by Jerry Yudelson.
      p. cm.
  ISBN-13: 978-0-9718955-7-7
  1. Sustainable buildings--Design and construction. 2. Sustainable architecture. 3. Buildings--Environmental engineering.
  4. Ecological houses. I. Title.
  TH880.Y63 2006
   658.4'083--dc22
                        2006016672

Published by:
National Association of Industrial and Office Properties
2201 Cooperative Way, Suite 300
Herndon, Va. 20171
www.naiop.org
800-666-6780

Cover design by Estasi Design, interior design by Colburnhouse

Printed in the United States

9th & Stewart Life Sciences Building, Seattle, developed by Touchstone Corporation. Photography by Ben Benschnider.

CONTENTS

ACKNOWLEDGMENTS

My wife Jessica Stuart Yudelson (and my Scottie Madhu) put up with the magnificent obsession to write this book, during many evenings and weekends of 2005 in Portland. Robert Fox of Cook+Fox Architects in New York generously updated me about the Bank of America Tower development. Susan Kaplan of Battery Park City Authority, New York City, took the time to give me a tour of the Solaire, the first LEED Gold certified apartment building. Bruce Fowle of FX FOWLE Architects, New York City, provided information on the Helena high-rise condo project.

My former colleagues at Green Building Services, Portland, provided some helpful information from their work on LEED-certified projects, as did Swinerton Builders, San Francisco. Thanks to Hamilton Hazelhurst, Vulcan Real Estate Development, for his time in discussing how a major developer tackles green development, and to Alison Jeffries, marketing director, for her information on specific projects. I also benefited from talking with Jim Goldman and Rod Wille of Turner Construction about the implementation of their company's green building program.

My friends at Gerding/Edlen Development in Portland shared a copy of an advertisement for their green development projects. Friends and colleagues in the green building design, development and construction business in Portland, Seattle, San Francisco, Vancouver and other places have always been there with helpful advice and solid information. Thanks to the reviewers who lent their expertise and especially to Karen Colburn for assembling the case studies and to Ellen Hirzy for her editorial guidance. Thanks also to Sheila Vertino and NAIOP for their vision and commitment in seeing this book through to publication.

J.Y.

ABOUT THE AUTHOR

Jerry Yudelson has been involved in marketing renewable energy systems, environmental remediation products and services, and green building design and consulting services for more than 25 years. His work has been motivated by a desire to make a difference, to work with many others toward a more healthy way to exist together on this one planet Earth.

Jerry has worked with real estate firms, state government, utilities, local governments, Fortune 500 companies, small businesses, engineering firms and product manufacturers as a marketing specialist. He holds an MBA with highest honors from the University of Oregon and taught 60 MBA-level courses in marketing, business planning, organizational development and public relations. A registered professional engineer in Oregon, he holds degrees in civil and environmental engineering from Caltech and Harvard. He has been the marketing director for two mid-sized building engineering firms serving the design and construction industry, and in 2000 he cofounded one of the largest green building consulting groups in the country. He has been a management consultant to more than 75 CEOs of various-sized firms and a marketing consultant to more than 100 companies.

Currently, as associate principal and sustainability director for a mid-sized consulting engineering firm based in Portland, he works for developers and design teams seeking LEED (Leadership in Energy and Environmental Design) certification of projects. His work on design projects involves early-stage consulting, charrette facilitation and serving as a LEED expert and coach for design teams.

In addition to this general business and professional background, Jerry has served as a LEED Workshop national faculty member for the U.S. Green Building Council (USGBC). Since 2001, he has trained more than 2,000 building industry professionals in nine states and two Canadian provinces in the LEED system. He has served on the USGBC's national board of directors and currently chairs the steering committee for the USGBC's annual conference, *Greenbuild*, the largest green building conference in the world, to be held in Denver in November 2006. Jerry also serves on the committee charged with producing the LEED for Core and Shell standard for the development community.

In 2004, the Northwest Energy Efficiency Alliance, through its Better Bricks program, named him Green Building Advocate of the Year, and the *Sustainable Industries Journal* named him one of the top 25 leaders of the green building industry. He serves on the editorial boards of a national trade journal, *Environmental Design & Construction*, and *The Marketer*, published by the Society for Marketing Professional Services.

PREFACE

This book describes the practice of marketing green developments. It is designed for professionals whose livelihood depends on financing, building and marketing development projects; selling design and construction services; operating developments with green features; and specifying systems to serve these requirements — all of whom are trying to transform the building and development industry into a more environmentally responsible and energy-efficient activity.

According to Tom Watson, the marketing genius who built IBM, nothing happens until a sale is made. Green building designers and developers need a firm grounding in marketing theory and contemporary marketing strategy and tactics to be effective in this rapidly changing marketplace. Marketers and executives for conventional developers need to understand what the green building client really wants and how to be more effective in presenting green design features, sustainable strategies and new products to this type of buyer.

The following chapters raise several key questions: How is green building and green development marketing similar to other types of real estate marketing, and how is it different? What conventional marketing tools and techniques can we use in marketing green buildings and green developments? What is the actual (and potential) size of the market for green buildings and green developments? How can we estimate the future growth of this market? Who are the winners so far in green building marketing? How should a firm position itself to succeed in this growing marketplace?

Throughout the text, I rely on published data, current through early 2006. Most of this information is available publicly from the U.S. Green Building Council, from papers at green building conferences or from trade magazines. I have conducted and reviewed a number of proprietary surveys, and I have benefited from many personal interviews to round out the picture of green developments in the United States.

I am relying on NAIOP members, other developers and users of this information, and green development professionals to transform the building and development industry into one that produces what most people say they want from it: energy- and resource-efficient, environmentally sound, healthy, comfortable and productive places to live, work, learn, experiment and recreate. Thanks for your interest in this book, and profitable reading! I welcome any feedback, directed to me at my personal e-mail address: jyudelson@cox.net, or via my personal Web site, www.yudelson.net.

Jerry Yudelson, PE, MS, MBA, LEED AP
Portland, Oregon and Tucson, Arizona
April 2006

Calamos Investments Headquarters, Naperville, Illinois, developed by Calamos Real Estate LLC.

MAKING THE BUSINESS CASE FOR GREEN BUILDINGS

Owners and developers of commercial and institutional properties across North America are discovering that it is often possible to build green buildings on conventional budgets or with minor cost premiums. Many developers, building owners and facility managers are advancing the state of the art in commercial buildings through new modeling tools, design techniques, advanced green products and creative use of financial and regulatory incentives. For the past 10 years, in ever-increasing numbers, we have seen development of commercial structures for owner-built, built-to-suit and speculative purposes using green building techniques and technologies.

With more than half of the world's 500 largest corporations issuing sustainability reports in 2005, it is clear that this market will not be a short-lived fad. Companies want to build and occupy real estate that reflects their values, and a high-performance building goes a long way toward satisfying that requirement.[1]

Most long-time observers of the real estate, architectural design and building construction industries say that sustainable design is the biggest sea change in their business careers. The urgency of global warming and the increasing U.S. dependence on expensive imported energy have led architects to urge more concerted action on energy use in buildings. In late 2005, the American Institute of Architects, representing more than 100,000 U.S. architects, issued a major new policy that set a goal of reducing the fossil fuel consumption of new buildings by 50 percent by the year 2010, with additional 10 percent reductions every five years thereafter. While this declaration has no legal force, it does add pressure to incorporate superior energy performance into the goals for each project.[2] As architect Edward Mazria observed, you can achieve a 50 percent reduction with existing building technology at no extra cost by simply using the right design strategies, such as daylighting and passive heating and cooling techniques.[3]

UNDERSTANDING GREEN BUILDINGS

What do we mean when we speak of green buildings or high-performance buildings? According to the U.S. Green Building Council, these buildings incorporate design and construction practices that significantly reduce or eliminate the negative impact of buildings on the environment and occupants in five broad areas:

- Sustainable site planning
- Safeguarding water and water efficiency
- Energy efficiency and renewable energy
- Conservation of materials and resources
- Indoor environmental quality.[4]

Typically, such buildings are measured against code buildings — structures that qualify for a building permit but do not exceed minimum requirements. In addition, green buildings are often measured according to a system such as the LEED rating system (www.usgbc.org), the Collaborative for High-Performance Schools (CHPS) ratings (www.chps.net), the Advanced Building™ guidelines (www.poweryourdesign.com), or in some cases local utility or city guidelines (a number of utilities have rating systems for residential buildings, for example). Such buildings typically must score a minimum number of points above the code threshold to qualify for a rating of green, certified or high-performance.

Since the introduction of LEED in the spring of 2000, it has become for all practical purposes the U.S. national standard. LEED is primarily a performance standard; in other words, it generally allows a developer or owner to choose how to meet certain benchmark numbers — saving 20 percent on energy use versus code, for example — without prescribing specific measures. In this way, LEED is a flexible tool for evaluating new construction or major renovations in almost all commercial, institutional and high-rise residential buildings throughout North America. Canada has an almost identical version of LEED, but at this time there is no Mexican version.[5] Since its inception, LEED has proven its value as a design tool for architectural teams tasked with creating green buildings, and more than 3,000 projects have registered their intention to use LEED.

LEED provides for four levels of certification: Certified, Silver, Gold and Platinum. In 2003 and 2004, three projects in southern California achieved the Platinum rating: one project for a local utility, another for a county park with the Audubon Society and another for the Natural Resources Defense Council. As of April 2006, the largest Platinum project was the Cambridge, Massachusetts, headquarters of Genzyme Corporation, at about 360,000 square feet. (See Case Studies on CD for more about Genzyme Center, developed by Lyme Properties, LLC.) By March of 2006, nearly 350 projects had completed the certification process under LEED for New Construction (LEED-NC). The author predicts that more than 300 new buildings will be certified in 2006.

WHO IS USING LEED?

By the end of 2005, LEED had captured about 3 percent of the total new building market, with about 2,800 registered projects encompassing more than 350 million square feet of new and renovated space. Currently, nearly 100 new projects per month are registering for evaluation under LEED. Since a new or renovated building can only be LEED-certified after it is ready for occupancy, many projects are just nearing completion of their documentation for a LEED rating. Given that it often takes two years or more for projects to move from design to completion (and certification can only take place after substantial completion of a project), marketers should be pressuring their firms and their clients now to step up and participate in the certification of existing or upcoming projects.

Just about every conceivable project type has been LEED-registered, including a mostly underground Oregon winemaking facility! For example, the first 50 LEED Gold project certifications included such varied building types as:

- Renovation of a 100-year-old warehouse in Portland, Oregon
- A developer-driven technology park in Victoria, British Columbia (see case study)
- An office-warehouse building in Gresham, Oregon
- A nonprofit office building in Menlo Park, California
- A new office building and an office building renovation for Herman Miller, Inc., in Zeeland, Michigan (see case study)
- A public office building leased to the Commonwealth of Pennsylvania by a developer
- A large state office building in Sacramento, California
- An environmental learning center near Seattle, Washington

case study ———————————————————————

Leading the Way to Gold

Victoria, British Columbia: Vancouver Island Technology Park

This project, completed in 2001 and awarded the first LEED-NC Gold certification in Canada in 2002, was a public developer-driven project by the British Columbia Buildings Corporation that upgraded an abandoned 165,000-square-foot, 1970s hospital building into a modern office building. Energy consumption was cut by more than 30 percent over a conventional building.[6] This project reused 100 percent of the existing structure and 91 percent of the existing shell. The renovation budget was $11.9 million Canadian, or about $72 per square foot (about $50 to $52 U.S. per square foot). Annual energy savings are estimated at $50,000 Canadian, or about 30 cents per square foot, a reduction of about 27 percent from a conventional building (remember that this is a renovation, and most of the exterior walls and glazing were not changed).

Zeeland, Michigan: Herman Miller Marketplace

Completed in January 2002, this two-story, 95,000-square-foot speculative office building, owned by The Granger Group, is typically occupied by 430 people and received a LEED-NC Gold rating. It was built for $89 per square foot ($8.5 million, excluding land) and is expected to reduce energy costs by 40 percent compared with a conventional building. Operating cost savings are estimated at $1 million over a 7-year lease. Annual energy use is estimated at 29 kwh per square foot, or about $2.90 at 10 cents per kwh, in a harsh northern climate. The exterior walls are more than 60 percent glazing, which hurts energy use but promotes extensive daylighting.

Of the first 42 LEED Gold projects, 13 (31 percent) were corporate projects, while the balance were public agency, educational and nonprofit in nature. This split suggests that some immediate impacts of LEED will be on developers who provide build-to-suit projects for the public sector, corporate facility managers responding to sustainability mandates, and speculative developments in certain markets.

INCENTIVES AND BARRIERS TO GREEN DEVELOPMENT

Senior executives representing architectural/engineering firms, consultants, developers, building owners, corporate owner-occupants and educational institutions have positive attitudes about the benefits and costs of green construction, according to the 2005 Green Building Market Barometer, a survey conducted by Turner Construction Company.[7] When asked to compare green buildings with traditional construction, the respondents agreed that for little or no additional cost, green construction yields greater benefits in terms of:

- occupants' health and well-being (88 percent);
- building value (84 percent);
- worker productivity (78 percent) and
- return on investment (68 percent).

Fifty-seven percent of the 665 executives surveyed said their companies are involved with green buildings; 83 percent said their green building workload had increased since 2002; and 87 percent said they expected green building activity to continue. Thirty-four percent of those not currently working with green construction said their organization would be likely to do so over the next three years.

Given these positive views, it is surprising that the top obstacles to widespread adoption of green building approaches are perceived higher costs (68 percent) and lack of awareness regarding the benefits of green construction (64 percent). Other factors discouraging green construction are the perceived complexity and cost of LEED documentation (54 percent), short-term corporate budget horizons (51 percent), long payback (50 percent), the difficulty in quantifying the benefits (47 percent) and the more complex construction involved (30 percent).

FOUR WAYS TO OVERCOME THE BARRIERS

Looking at the issues raised in the Turner Construction survey from a marketing perspective, it's clear that green building developers must make the business case for a product that appears to cost more, doesn't demonstrate significant tangible benefits to balance the costs, and is being sold to a group that is very concerned about initial cost increases.

As a developer, you have four possible solutions:

1. *Work aggressively to lower the costs of building green* through your own project experience and a focus on integrated design approaches that might lower some costs (such as HVAC systems) while increasing others (such as building envelope insulation and better glazing), but with a net positive cost impact.

2. *Develop communication and marketing strategies* that make good use of the available research that demonstrates the benefits of green buildings in order to justify the economic and market risks inherent in trying something new.

3. *Find ways to finance green building improvements* to reduce or eliminate the first-cost penalty that often frightens away prospective buyers, using incentives from utilities and local, state and federal governments to maximize points of leverage. (See Case Studies on CD for details on how developers such as Heffner and Weber targeted Smart Growth and Priority Funding areas for green development.)

4. *Study and try to duplicate the successful project results for institutional buyers* — 60 percent or more of the current market for LEED-registered buildings — that document the full range of green building benefits so that building owners with a long-term ownership perspective can be motivated to find the additional funds to build high-performance buildings.

As a developer, the more experience you have with green buildings, the better you are able to build a case —first within your company and then in the client's mind. Some clients will be inherently more convinced of the benefits of green buildings, less skeptical about their ability to achieve the desired results, and more willing to work with development teams to solve the problems that usually arise in trying new technologies and new approaches to building design.

BENEFITS THAT BUILD A BUSINESS CASE

The business case for green development is based on a framework of benefits: economic, productivity, risk management, and public relations and marketing.[8] This section outlines the framework. (See Case Studies on CD for information on how Corporate Office Properties Trust, NAIOP's 2005 Green Development Award Winner, put this framework into action with their LEED Gold-certified project in Annapolis Junction, Maryland.)

Chapter 6 provides more specific tools for making the business case: how to classify the value of green buildings, how to translate the benefits into a consistent set of buyer motivations and how to capture the financial benefits of green development.

case study

Resource Efficiency + Operational Savings = Good Business Sense

Seattle: Seattle Biomedical Research Institute (SBRI)

Completed in May 2004, this 112,000-square-foot, five-story speculative laboratory and office building was certified at LEED Silver under the LEED for Core and Shell program. Developed by Vulcan Inc., Harbor Properties and the Seattle Biomedical Research Institute, the project expects to reduce annual water consumption by 23 percent and to use 35 percent less energy than a conventional lab building ($43,000 annual savings, or 38 cents per square foot). The building includes large windows and design elements to promote daylighting. Ada Healy, vice president of real estate at Vulcan, a major downtown Seattle developer, says the building validates the business case for sustainable development: The operational savings and resource-efficient features translate to additional income that can be used to advance the research and business goals of tenants. SBRI occupies the top two floors of the building with its 200 researchers.[9] The project includes 10,000 square feet of ground-floor retail space. SBRI received $144,000 in incentive payments from Seattle City Light for energy conservation and $20,000 from the City of Seattle to offset LEED documentation costs. Having an environmentally conscious research facility helps attract employees who want to work in sustainable environments while showing that sustainable projects can build neighborhood connections with such elements as ground-floor retail.

Economic Benefits

Reduced operating costs. With the real price of oil predicted to stay above $54 per barrel (in 2005 dollars) for the next 20 years[10] and peak-period electricity prices rising steadily, energy-efficient buildings make good business sense. Even in triple-net leases in which the tenant pays all operating costs, landlords want to offer tenants the most economical space for their money. For a reasonable investment in capital cost, green buildings will save on energy operating costs for years to come. Many green buildings are designed to use 25 to 40 percent less energy than current codes require; some buildings achieve even higher efficiency levels. Translated to an operating cost of $1.60 to $2.50 per square foot for electricity (the most common fuel), this energy savings could reduce utility operating costs by $0.40 to $1.00 per year. Often these savings are achieved for an investment of just $1.00 to $3.00 per square foot. With building costs reaching $100 to $150 per square foot, it is a wise business decision to invest 1 to 2 percent of capital cost to secure long-term savings, particularly with a payback of less than three years. In an 80,000-square-foot building, the owner's savings translates into $32,000 to $80,000 per year.

Reduced maintenance costs. Energy-saving buildings that are properly commissioned at $0.50 to $1.00 per square foot of initial cost (equal to one year of savings) show additional savings of 10 to 15 percent in energy costs. They also tend to be much easier to operate and maintain.[11] By conducting comprehensive functional testing of all energy-using systems before occupancy, it is often possible to have a smoother-running building for years because potential problems are fixed in advance. A key part of the commissioning process is documenting operator training. In this way, new personnel can be trained to keep the facility running at peak efficiency.

Increased building value. Increased annual energy savings will also create higher building values. Imagine a building that saves $37,500 per year in energy costs versus a comparable building built to code (this savings might amount to $0.50 per year per square foot for a 75,000-square-foot building). At a capitalization rate (effective discount rate) of 8 percent, green building standards would add $468,750 ($6.25 per square foot) to the value of the building. For a small upfront investment, an owner can reap benefits that typically offer a payback of three years or less and an internal rate of return exceeding 20 percent, because it is nearly a sure bet that energy costs will continue to rise faster than the general rate of inflation and faster than rents can be increased.

Top-line revenue gains. Over the past ten years, American business has focused profit growth successfully on squeezing costs out of operations, through downsizing, right-sizing, outsourcing, logistics improvements, and so on. To grow profits now, companies need to grow top-line revenue. In the service economy, top-line revenue growth comes from recruiting and retaining top performers. The "80/20 rule" guarantees that 80 percent of revenues will come from 20 percent of people, so companies have focused a good part of their marketing strategies necessarily on the "blocking and tackling" of making their companies attractive to key people. Add to that the increasing scarcity of "Gen Xers" (28 to 41 years old in 2006) who occupy key project management and leadership roles (by 2010, their numbers will be 25 percent less in terms of economic activity than in 1995), and one can see why green buildings have increasing importance for companies. They represent one of the few measures for getting and keeping good people, especially those who drive top-line revenue growth. (Think of the importance, for example, of principals and senior associates in all manner of professional service firms — lawyers, accountants, architects, engineers — as well as in client contact and project leadership roles in finance, insurance and real estate.) This issue is now emerging as a key rationale for green building consideration by corporate America.

Productivity Benefits

In the service economy, productivity gains for healthier indoor spaces are worth anywhere from 1 to 5 percent of employee costs, or about $3.00 to $30.00 per square foot of leasable or usable space. This estimate is based on average costs of $300 to $600 per square foot per employee per year (based on $60,000 average annual salary and benefits and 100 to 200 square feet per person).[12] With energy costs typically under $2.50 per square foot per year, it appears that productivity gains may easily equal or exceed the entire energy cost of operating a building. Productivity gains from high-performance lighting in 11 studies averaged 3.2 percent, or about $2 to $6 per square foot per year, an amount equal to the cost of energy. For corporate and institutional owners and occupiers of buildings, that is too much of a savings to ignore. (See Case Studies on CD for details on why developers like Calamos Real Estate LLC chose a sustainable design for Calamos Investment's new corporate headquarters to attract and retain tomorrow's knowledge-based workers.)

Risk Management Benefits

Green building certification may provide some measure of future lawsuit protection through third-party certification of measures installed to protect indoor air quality, beyond just meeting code. With the national focus on mold and its effect on building occupants, developers and owners need to refocus their attention on indoor air quality.

Faster permitting or special permit assistance can also be considered a type of risk management. In Chicago, for example, the city government has created the position of green projects administrator and is allowing these projects to receive priority processing. For large projects that exceed minimum requirements, the city waives fees for independent code consultants. Projects with top-rated green goals are promised a permit review within 15 days.[13]

Public Relations and Marketing Benefits

Stakeholder relations and occupant satisfaction. Tenants and employees want to see a demonstrated concern for their well-being and for that of the planet. Savvy developers and owners are beginning to realize how to market these benefits to a discerning and skeptical client and stakeholder base using the advantages of green building certifications and other forms of documentation, including local utility and industry programs.

case study

Selling the Benefits to Tenants

Seattle: Alcyone Apartments

When the Alcyone Apartments in Seattle opened in the summer of 2004, the developers used the green features of the building as a prime selling point. This seven-story, 162-unit project is promoting a "laid-back lifestyle in an urban environment" in the Lake Union neighborhood near downtown. Leasing was completed in about nine months in a soft apartment market, with a broad age range of tenants. The three main selling points are the units themselves, the quiet location with neighborhood amenities and the focus on healthy living. The Web site (www.alcyoneapartments.com) features a description of the LEED system and the project's LEED certification, as well as a sustainability fact sheet that succinctly presents the green features and benefits of the project (Table 1.1).

Table 1.1
Sustainability Fact Sheet, Alcyone Apartments, Seattle, Washington

What we did	How residents will benefit
Commercial quality energy-efficient windows	More temperate spaces with increased natural light, greater thermal comfort and the potential for lower utility bills
A central gas-fired domestic hot water system	Reduced energy use, which means lower utility bills, versus individual water heaters in each apartment
Steel stud metal-gauge framing (instead of wood) to increase durability and eliminate shrinkage	Fewer leaks mean less chance of furniture or fixture damage due to water intrusion and mold contamination (a big issue in a cool, rainy climate such as Seattle)
Low volatile organic compound (VOC) paints and carpets limit the off-gassing of toxic chemical elements into the indoor air	Improved indoor air quality and a healthier indoor environment
Flexcar (hourly rental) parking spaces, electric vehicle charging stations and bicycle storage facilities encourage alternative transportation	Reduced demand for parking spaces among tenants and potential cost saving from not having to own or operate a car
A rooftop Pea Patch garden with recycled rainwater irrigation provides green space, reduces water consumption and mitigates stormwater runoff from the roof	A green space amenity with a rooftop garden where residents can grow their own plants
80 percent of construction waste was recycled to avoid landfill disposal	A sustainable living environment from design through construction
Located our project on a convenient urban site utilizing existing infrastructure	The convenience of reduced commute times, public transportation options and nearby culture and entertainment opportunities

Source: Alcyone Apartments Web site, www.alcyoneapartments.com

Being a good neighbor is appropriate not just for building users, but for the larger community. Developers and owners are beginning to see the marketing and public relations benefits (including branding) of a demonstrated concern for the environment.

Environmental stewardship. Many larger public and private organizations have well-articulated sustainability mission statements and are understanding how their real estate choices can both reflect and advance those missions. Writing in *Urban Land* magazine, developer Jonathan F. P. Rose notes that "having a socially and environmentally motivated mission makes it easier for businesses in the real estate industry to recruit, and retain, top talent. Communities are more likely to support green projects than traditional projects, and it is easier for such projects to qualify for many government contracts, subsidies, grants and tax credits. The real estate industry can prosper by making environmentally responsible decisions."[14]

More competitive product in the marketplace. Speculative developers are realizing that green buildings can be more competitive in certain markets if they can be built on a conventional budget. Whether for speculative or build-to-suit purposes, green buildings with lower operating costs and better indoor environmental quality should be more attractive to a growing group of corporate, public and individual buyers. Green-ness will not replace known attributes such as price, location and conventional amenities, but green features will increasingly enter into tenants' decisions about leasing space and into buyers' decisions about purchasing properties.

ENDNOTES

1.   According to the KPMG *International Survey of Corporate Sustainability Reporting 2002*, approximately 45 percent of the Global Fortune 250 now produces some type of social, environmental, corporate citizenship, or sustainability report. Mark Brownlie column, (October 2003), in www.greenbiz.com.

2.   Architectural Record, accessed 5/8/06: http://archrecord.construction.com/features/green/archives/051227aia.asp.

3.   Feb. 2006 Architectural Record, accessed 5/8/06: http://archrecord.construction.com/features/green/archives/060201mazria.asp: *How Architects Can Reverse Global Warming: A Conversation with Edward Mazria, AIA*

4.   USGBC Introductory PowerPoint Presentation on Green Buildings, available at www.usgbc.org/resources.

5.   See www.cagbc.org.

6.   Alison Northey, "Going for Gold," available at www.buildgreendevelopments.com/downloads/green_space.pdf.

7.   Available at www.turnerconstruction.com/greensurvey05.pdf.

8. U.S. Green Building Council, *Making the Business Case for High-Performance Green Buildings* (Washington, D.C.: U.S. Green Building Council, 2002), available at www.usgbc.org/resources/usbgc_brochures.asp. See also *Environmental Building News*, 14, no. 4 (April 2005), available at www.buildinggreen.com.

9. Press release, Vulcan, Inc., Feb. 9, 2005; *Seattle Daily Journal of Commerce*, July 28, 2005 (www.djc.com) and U.S. Green Building Council case study.

10. See www.eia.doe.gov/oiaf/aeo/key.html for the November 2005 forecast.

11. See the recent meta-study by Lawrence Berkeley National Laboratory, *The Cost-Effectiveness of Commercial-Buildings Commissioning*, available at http://eetd.lbl.gov/emills/PUBS/Cx-Costs-Benefits.html. This research reviewed 224 studies of the benefits of building commissioning and concluded that based on energy savings alone, such investments have a payback within five years.

12. Eleven case studies have shown that innovative daylighting systems can pay for themselves in less than one year due to energy and productivity benefits. Vivian Loftness et al., *Building Investment Decision Support* (BIDS™) (Pittsburgh: Center for Building Performance and Diagnostics, Carnegie Mellon University, n.d.), available at http://cbpd.arc.cmu.edu/ebids.

13. "Speedy Permitting Has Developers Turning Green in Chicago," *Building Design & Construction*, November 2005, p. 28; available at www.BDCnetwork.com.

14. Jonathan F. P. Rose, "The Business Case for Green Building," *Urban Land*, June 2005, p. 71; available at www.uli.org.

Georgia Institute of Technology's Technology Square, development managed by Jones Lang LaSalle. Photography by Brian Gassel of Thompson, Ventulett, Stainback & Associates, Inc.

CURRENT MARKET TRENDS FOR GREEN BUILDINGS

The green building industry in the United States has seen significant expansion in this decade. By the end of 2005, the LEED green building rating system — a good indicator of green building activity — had captured about 3 percent of the market for new commercial and institutional buildings, with about 2,800 registered projects encompassing more than 350 million square feet of new and renovated green building space (see Fig. 2.1). LEED-NC project registrations in 2005 topped 1,000 for the first time, adding more than 130 million gross square feet of project area.

Many states and municipalities have adopted green building policies, incentives, laws and regulations, as support for green building spreads across the country. At the federal level, the Energy Policy Act of 2005 (EPACT) provides increased incentives for solar and wind power along with strong support for energy conservation in new and existing buildings. Most observers expect Congress to extend EPACT beyond its scheduled expiration at the end of 2007.

Figure 2.1
Green Building Activity, 2000–2005[5]

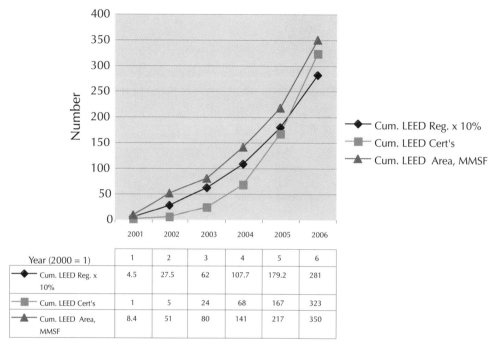

Year (2000 = 1)	1	2	3	4	5	6
Cum. LEED Reg. x 10%	4.5	27.5	62	107.7	179.2	281
Cum. LEED Cert's	1	5	24	68	167	323
Cum. LEED Area, MMSF	8.4	51	80	141	217	350

U.S. Green Building Council published data, assembled by Jerry Yudelson.

Professional organizations continue to promote green development as good business and responsible corporate citizenship. The number of LEED Accredited Professionals (LEED APs) exceeds 23,000; some large architectural firms now have more than 500 LEED APs on staff. The U.S. Green Building Council's annual *Greenbuild* conference — the largest conference and trade show of its kind in the world — attracted nearly 10,000 participants to Atlanta in November 2005. The American Institute of Architects issued its most ambitious policy statement supporting sustainable design, declaring in December 2005 that by 2010, current consumption levels in new buildings should decrease by 50 percent.

Changing public demand is influencing this move toward green development. For all the reasons described in Chapter 1, green buildings make good business sense, especially as global political and environmental conditions prompt rising concerns about the future.

Oil prices are increasing, and the current geopolitical situation intensifies the prospect of uncertain supplies in the coming years. The price per barrel surged above $50 per barrel in 2005 — and to $75 in April 2006 — and threatened to stay at that level. The U.S. Energy Information Administration's annual long-term forecast for 2025 estimated oil at $54 per barrel in 2005 dollars, up 65 percent from its 2004 estimate. Growing evidence for human-induced global warming also makes people uneasy about dwindling natural resources. Both factors have prompted a stronger public acceptance of the need for conserving fossil fuel-generated energy in buildings and in urban design in general.

The lifestyle preferences of 21st-century consumers also bring new demand for green buildings. More people — especially among the huge wave of retiring baby boomers — are choosing to "reurbanize" in healthy, environmentally friendly settings. Consumers in the LOHAS (Lifestyles of Health and Sustainability) category — identified as "Cultural Creatives" by Paul H. Ray and Sherry Ruth Anderson — constitute 37 percent of the population. These educated consumers make conscientious purchasing and investing decisions based on social and cultural values. They represent a powerful $228.9 billion marketplace for sustainable goods and services, with an estimated $76.47 billion to spend in the sustainable economy market sector on green building, renewable energy, and other items.[1]

A recent survey conducted for the U.S. Green Building Council projected near-term market growth in green construction for the following building sectors:

- Education — 65 percent
- Government — 62 percent
- Institutional — 54 percent
- Office — 48 percent
- Health care — 46 percent
- Residential — 32 percent
- Hospitality — 22 percent
- Retail — 20 percent[2]

From a developer's point of view, it makes sense to study market trends in several ways:

- the current market impact of green buildings by geography, project type and owner type
- growth trends based on LEED data
- the vertical markets that developers should consider

CURRENT MARKET IMPACT

Geography

Geographically, the top 10 states for LEED project registrations at the end of 2005 were:

1. California (433 projects)
2. New York (164)
3. Washington (162)
4. Pennsylvania (155)

5. Oregon (121)
6. Texas (107)
7. Illinois (107)
8. Michigan (105)
9. Georgia (93)
10. Massachusetts (92)[3]

On a per-capita basis, small states such as Oregon and Washington lead the way (see Table 5.1, page 53). Oregon has about 3.3 times the national average project registrations per capita, and Washington has about 2.7 times the average. California, in contrast, is just 1.2 times the national average in registered projects per capita, a surprising fact given that state's strong environmental advocacy on many other issues. Including British Columbia project registrations in the total would make it clear that the west coast has more than 25 percent of all LEED project registrations, with only about 16 percent of the total U.S. and Canadian population. Other areas of heightened interest include the Great Lakes area, Texas and the New England-New York-mid-Atlantic area.

Project Type

LEED registrations by project type are a bit harder to discern, because USGBC data groups many projects into a multiple-use category. With this caveat, the project types with the largest number of LEED-NC registrations are the following, excluding multiple use:

- Commercial office (21 percent)
- Schools and colleges (19 percent)
- Public order/safety (7 percent)
- Multifamily residential (6 percent)[4]

LEED is now widespread in the commercial office category and fairly widespread in schools and colleges. A large number of mostly public projects represent the next level of activity (assembly, interpretive center, library and public order-safety such as police and fire stations, as well as courthouses). Obviously, the public sector also represents much of the commercial office project type as well. Two interesting areas for future growth are multifamily residential, in which marketing advantages are gradually appearing, and industrial, likely driven by corporate sustainability policies.

Owner Type

In this segment, the classifications are easier to understand, possibly because they are fewer in number and more readily classified by type (see Table 2.1 and Fig. 2.2).

Table 2.1
Growth of LEED-Registered Projects by Owner Type, 2003–2005

Owner Type	July 2003 Projects	July 2004 Projects	September 2005 Projects	% of Total Projects, 2005	% Growth, 2003–2004	% Growth, 2004–2005
For-profit corporation	237	372	579	26	57	56
Local government	227	345	494	23	52	43
Nonprofit corporation	138	272	441	20	97	62
State government	100	174	260	12	74	49
Federal government	81	142	188	9	75	32
Other	51	109	179	8	115	64
Individual	7	14	36	2	100	157
Total projects	841	1,428	2,177		70	52

Source: U.S. Green Building Council published data assembled by Jerry Yudelson. Nonprofits include private schools and colleges.

Figure 2.2
LEED-Registered Projects by Owner Type, through January 2006

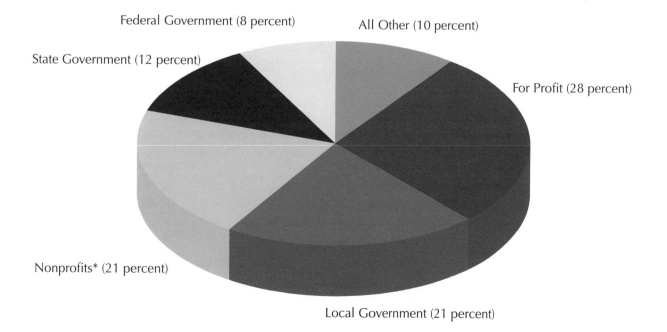

Source: USGBC, current through January 2006. Nonprofits include private schools and colleges.

Government

From this information, it is clear that government, nonprofit and institutional users (including education and health care) have dominated the first five years of LEED project registrations, with 64 percent of the total registrations and 54 percent of the total registered project area (excluding other/individual project registrations for which no owner type is specified). Indeed, government-owned projects represent close to half (44 percent) of all LEED-registered projects to date, indicating the prevalence of two driving forces in the green building marketplace: long-term ownership and operations perspective, and environmental policy considerations. (These two considerations probably also are driving the nonprofit and corporate sector LEED registrations.)

What does this situation mean for developers? One implication is that a focus on government and institutional build-to-suit projects may be warranted, since these projects are likely to have strong policies driving their use of the LEED rating system for project evaluation. A second implication is that larger private-sector companies that are more likely to have sustainability or environmental stewardship policies and aspirations are also potentially valid targets. The facilities and corporate real estate groups are often divorced from larger corporate goals and primarily concerned with lowering real estate costs for building projects, making the green building sell a bit harder to accomplish if it raises initial costs.

This attitude is changing, however, as the business case for productivity increases and other soft benefits in green buildings (see Chapter 6), particularly the effects of daylighting, higher indoor air quality levels and views to the outdoors, start to be more appreciated.

Higher Education

According to LEED statistics, higher-education project registrations represent about 7 percent of the first 2,800 projects, through the end of 2005, or about 200 total projects, encompassing the entire range of building types and uses. Through the first six years of the program, such LEED registrations averaged about 30 per year, for the nearly 3,000 colleges and universities in the U.S., representing obviously less than one percent of the higher education building market. As of September 2005, 44 of these projects had been certified. The author's own survey of campuses shows that at least 50 percent of LEED projects through 2004 existed because of support from top leadership. However, based on the author's professional experience, the campus environment across the U.S. is rapidly moving to embrace sustainability as an organizing principle for research, teaching, operations and facilities. One marker of this trend is the formation in 2005 of a new umbrella organization, the Association for the Advancement of Sustainability in Higher Education (www.aashe.org) that is rapidly growing in university membership. At Arizona State University, president Michael Crow has made sustainability a core organizing principle and has created an Office of Sustainability Initiatives with a $15 million endowment. Look for this trend to bring LEED Silver or better requirements for new facilities at most universities within the next five years.[6]

Higher Education Demonstrates its Commitment to Alternative Energy Technologies

Muskegon, Michigan: Grand Valley State University

The LEED Gold-certified, 26,000-square-foot Michigan Alternative and Renewable Energy Center (MAREC) serves as a business incubator and a research and development center, as well as a major demonstration project for alternative energy technologies. The center was completed by Workstage LLC, a corporate and institutional turnkey green developer based in Grand Rapids, Michigan. Just as the center is poised for changes in the energy industry, the building has been designed to accommodate future technology changes. It features a state-of-the-art operating platform called the Stage, which integrates HVAC, voice, data and electrical cabling under a raised floor. Housing these systems at floor level allows quick and easy access to all utilities so that changes in technology or space happen in hours instead of days. The flexibility gives Grand Valley State University a forward-thinking facility for its cutting-edge research.[7]

In addition to creating the sustainable structure, Workstage leveraged its relationship with Steelcase to implement a work environment using Steelcase's user-centered furniture design and space planning.

Higher education may not seem like a developers' market, but most campuses do not have the funds to build all the facilities they need and are increasingly turning to developers for funding, project management, ownership and operations. Most campuses still will be in business 50 or 100 years from now, so they make excellent captive tenants. (See the Case Studies CD for a profile on how the Georgia Institute of Technology revitalized midtown Atlanta with its Technology Square campus, developed by Jones Lang LaSalle.)

Private Sector

The 26 percent of LEED-registered projects in the private sector shown in Table 2.1 have widely varying ownership types and perspectives. Many of the initial projects have come from large corporations that have strong environmental stewardship goals and values and wanted to walk the talk in their (typically large) building projects. These companies include Ford, Toyota, Honda, The Gap, Goldman Sachs and PNC Bank. In addition, many small business owners (including architects designing their own facilities) have strong core environmental values that they want to illustrate in their own, typically smaller, projects. Finally, a few speculative developers have decided that LEED is the right thing to do and have found that LEED goals and registration can confer marketing advantages.

Table 2.2
Growth of LEED-Registered Projects by Area, 2003–2005

Owner Type	July 2003 (000 sq. ft.)	July 2005 (000 sq. ft.)	Average Project Size (000) Sq. Ft., 2004	Average Project Size (000) Sq. Ft., 2005	% of Total Project Area, 2005	% Growth, Project Area, 2004–2005 (15 mos.)
For-profit corporation	37,399	87,697	157.4	151.4	35	49.9
Local government	24,381	45,237	94.3	91.6	18	39.0
Nonprofit corporation	14,583	35,574	90.8	80.7	14	44.0
State government	16,397	29,827	134.6	114.7	12	27.4
Federal government	12,666	24,817	152.7	132.0	10	14.3
Other	5,938	21,791	138.5	121.7	9	44.4
Individual	410	2,547	55.4	70.8	1	228.0
Total project area	111,774	247,493				40.0
Average project size (000 sq. ft)	132.9		123.8	113.7		-8.2

Source: USGBC, September 2005, July 20, 2004, and July 31, 2003, data tallied by Jerry Yudelson

LEED GROWTH TRENDS

Growth by Owner Type

The greatest growth in projects by owner type occurred in the nonprofit sector, followed by the private sector; federal, state and local government projects grew more slowly than the average (Table 2.1). Although 44 percent of the registered projects through mid-2005 were in the government sector, the growth rate in that sector was below average. The percentage of for-profit LEED-registered projects is increasing slightly, as is that of nonprofit projects. At the end of 2005, for-profit owners accounted for only 28 percent of the total number of LEED projects but for about 35 percent of all LEED project areas, as these projects tend to be larger than others.

Growth by Project Size

For-profit companies tend to build larger projects — an average of about 151,000 square feet (based on 579 registered projects) — compared with an average of 100,000 square feet for all other projects (Table 2.2). At about $110 to $140 per square foot, the estimated construction cost of these projects would range from $16 million to $22 million. Federal projects represent the next largest average project size, at about 132,000 square feet each (based on 188 projects). State government projects on average are about 115,000 square feet, while the nonprofit and local government sectors build the smallest projects on average, except those owned by individuals. This difference is somewhat logical, given that local governments and nonprofits tend to build museums, recreation and cultural centers, libraries, fire and police stations, animal care facilities and similar smaller projects. By contrast, the for-profit and federal government sectors tend to build larger office buildings (134,000 square feet), laboratories (139,000 square feet), multiple-use (111,000 square feet) and similar facilities (Table 2.3).

Table 2.3
Growth of LEED-Registered Projects by Building Type, 2003–2005

Building Type	July 2003	September 2005	% of Total Projects, 2005	Average Size (000) Sq. Ft., 2005	% Growth, by Number, 2004–2005
Multiple-use	160	672	30.8	111	95
Commercial office	151	318	14.6	134	42
Higher education	84	155	7.1	79	34
K–12 education	52	133	6.1	121	60
Public order/safety	49	104	4.8	96	46
Multiunit residential	32	97	4.4	147	52
Interpretive center	45	77	3.5	28	18
Library	33	76	3.5	49	43
Industrial	33	71	3.2	140	29
Laboratory	27	52	2.4	140	13
Health care	19	45	2.1	276	55
Assembly	14	31	1.4	169	35
Recreation	11	30	1.4	43	25
Finance & communications	9	25	1.1	24	56
Retail	4	19	0.9	72	72
Military base	3	17	0.8	57	42
Transportation stations	9	16	0.7	310	45
Animal care	7	12	0.5	41	9
All other	99	235	10.8	N/A	39
Total	841	2,185		113	53

Source: USGBC, September 2005, July 20, 2004, and July 31, 2003, data tallied by Jerry Yudelson

Growth by Building Type

The largest category of LEED-registered buildings is multiple-use facilities, which might contain offices, parking and ground-floor retail (Table 2.3). These buildings accounted for nearly 31 percent of all LEED projects as of mid-2005. Government projects make up 38 percent of all projects by area and 44 percent of all projects, so they are being built at an average size of about 106,000 square feet (with construction costs in the $10 million to $15 million range). Among LEED-registered projects, the faster-growing building types are multiple-use, K-12 education, retail, multiunit residential and health care.

It is interesting that the growth of commercial office projects by project size was only half the growth by number, reflecting a smaller project size of 134,000 square feet for new registrants. This difference probably reflects the growth of smaller office buildings in the nonprofit and local government sectors as well as the increase in smaller private-owner buildings. The average size of new private-sector projects registered under LEED by mid-2005 was 151,000 square feet, showing that the private sector continues to build large projects. Not all are commercial or corporate offices; they include large multifamily housing projects, laboratories, and health care and industrial facilities. (See Case Studies on CD for a profile of a mixed-use project that bucked economic trends — Touchstone Corporation's 9th & Stewart Life Sciences Building in Seattle.)

VERTICAL MARKETS FOR GREEN BUILDINGS

A *vertical market* refers to a type of building use, while a *horizontal market* refers to technologies, such as solar energy, that could be used in a variety of building types. Vertical markets for green buildings — including commercial offices, higher education facilities and public facilities that might be accessible to developers — exist in every region, so it makes sense to look at how these markets view green buildings and how marketers are trying to address their needs.

It pays to remember two key facts when addressing green building markets: as of the end of 2005 relatively few architects had designed a LEED-certified building, and even fewer developers had built or sold one. A few building owners and developers are now specifying in their requests for proposals that a building project must achieve a LEED rating, but only a relative handful of government agencies are demanding a LEED Silver or Gold rating. Less frequently, some nonprofits are even going so far as to specify that a new project has to achieve a Platinum rating.

Commercial and Office Construction

According to U.S. Department of Commerce data, commercial and office construction represented a $115 billion market (annualized) in 2005, with offices accounting for $45 billion. According to USGBC data by building type (September 2005), 15 percent of LEED-registered

case study

Mixed-Use on a Grand Scale

Portland, Oregon: The Brewery Blocks

This five-block development on the site of the old Blitz-Weinhard brewery contains two office-commercial mixed-use towers, a condominium tower and an apartment tower, as well as an 1890s armory converted into a performing arts center (scheduled to open in Fall 2006). The 15-story condominium tower, the Henry, is certified at LEED Gold. The 16-story apartment tower, the Louisa, also is on track for LEED Silver certification in 2006. The other two blocks are successful office towers with ground-floor retail uses. The project has a four-block, three-level underground parking garage and a central chilled water plant serving the entire development.

Block 4, the M Financial Plaza, is a 241,000-square-foot, 10-story building completed in 2003, providing market-rate, Class-A commercial office space, with an estimated 24 percent annual energy savings. The building includes operable windows (a huge hit with tenants) and a green roof that captures and treats half the rainwater falling on the building. The project expects to receive a Silver LEED-NC certification in 2006. This building successfully leased in a very soft local real estate climate in 2003 and 2004. Among the first-in-town retailers it attracted for the ground-floor retail component were P.F. Chang's China Bistro and Anthropologie.[8]

Block 4 earned a 3-1 floor area ratio (FAR) bonus for covering the building's podium (setback) with an eco-roof and a 40-1 FAR bonus for installing bike storage, shower and locker facilities in the garage. Both strategies also earn LEED credits for urban heat island reduction and alternative transportation measures. A restrictive covenant preserving a neighboring historic armory allowed the transfer of that site's development rights to the other buildings on the property. In the end, the eco-roof, bike accommodations and historic preservation enabled the developer to add three floors to the building's tower (an extra 45 feet in height).

In terms of energy use, all chilled water, electricity and gas are submetered to retail and larger office tenants to encourage energy accountability and conservation. Modeled energy consumption is about 20 kilowatt-hours per square foot per year, or about $1.50 per square foot, at Portland's relatively cheap electricity rates of 7.5 cents per kwh.

projects were commercial offices, and 31 percent were multiple-use, a category that includes commercial offices or housing with ground-floor retail, parking garages or other uses. Of the first 246 LEED-certified projects listed on the USGBC Web site as of October 2005, 78 (32 percent) appear to be some form of office project.

Clearly, the market for LEED projects is still highly concentrated in the easiest market to approach, office buildings. Certification of an office building project is easy and fairly inexpensive, with most projects receiving 20 or more LEED points just in their initial basic design (out of 26 points needed for basic certification). LEED Silver certification costs might run $100,000 to $200,000 for a typical 100,000-square-foot building, including documentation, energy modeling and building commissioning, or about $1.00 to $2.00 per square foot. Cost premiums for basic LEED-certified buildings might be even less.

A good example is the IBM Tivoli Systems headquarters office in Austin, Texas, completed in January 2002, which received 26 points, the bare minimum needed to certify under LEED. The project is a five-story urban office building with 200,000 square feet of space, serving about 750 people. According to the project case study, green strategies added about 3 percent to the building's core construction cost, compared with IBM's normal building standards. Given that this building was designed in 2000, before architects and engineers were familiar with the LEED system and before all the bugs in the system had been worked out, a similar building today would show little or no construction cost premium to meet the basic LEED certification requirements. A project of this size would usually involve a cost of about $0.50 to $1.00 per square foot for meeting LEED technical requirements, including energy modeling and building commissioning, and for LEED certification documentation.

About 37 percent (17 out of 46) of the first commercial office projects certified under LEED were built by or for public agencies, slightly below the 44 percent share of all registered projects belonging to local, state or federal government agencies. Adding public safety facilities and most cultural and recreational projects (15 total) would bring the share of the initial 102 certified projects belonging to public agencies closer to the percentage of registered projects of this owner type. (One explanation for the discrepancy between publicly owned, registered and certified projects might also lie in the way the USGBC database treats higher education projects.) Including the nine publicly owned schools and universities would bring the number of publicly owned or publicly used certified projects to 40 percent of the total. Another explanation is that public agencies have stepped up their commitment to LEED in the past four years and that many of their projects are still in construction or in the midst of the certification process, so that an examination of the database at the end of 2005 indicates that publicly owned or publicly occupied LEED-certified projects are nearly 45 percent of the total.

Developers and builders of green commercial offices should be aware of and connected to the public agency market, which will likely represent nearly one-third to one-half of all commercial offices to be built to LEED standards in the next few years. Another good reason for staying on top of this market is that many public agencies are adopting LEED-friendly policies for their new commercial building projects.

Education

The value of educational construction exceeded $75 billion (annualized) in 2005.[9] Imagine that this market consists of 5,000 to 10,000 buildings valued at $7.5 million to $15 million each. Now further imagine that eventually 1,250 to 2,500 of those will be LEED-registered each year, given that LEED aims to address the top 25 percent of the market in each building sector. Therefore, in 2005, we estimate that about 14 percent of all LEED-registered projects were from the education market segment, or about 140 projects (14 percent of 1,000 newly registered projects), representing a 6 to 10 percent penetration of the ultimately accessible market for LEED education projects. Using the terminology of diffusion of innovations theory, this market is now clearly in the early adopter phase, with signs of accelerating growth in 2006.

Turner Construction's green building survey for 2005 specifically addressed the education market.[10] In summer 2005, Turner surveyed about 650 executives involved with schools and colleges. The importance of this market is indicated by the fact that school districts are estimated to spend $6 billion per year on energy costs. Clearly, the energy-saving aspects of green buildings are of critical importance to schools today and will be even more so in coming years.

For K-12 schools, more than 70 percent of those surveyed by Turner rated green buildings higher on community image, ability to attract and retain teachers, reduced student absenteeism and student performance. The greatest obstacles to green construction are the perceived higher costs (cited by 74 percent of the survey respondents) and lack of awareness of their benefits (67 percent). The main issue with incorporating more green features in educational construction, assuming that they cost more, is the separation of capital from operating budgets and the difficulty of incorporating life-cycle cost considerations in initial project budgets. This problem leads to short-term thinking, manifested in a desire to keep capital costs as low as possible. The challenge for developers in these markets is to figure out how to get greener buildings without increasing initial costs, or to convince decisionmakers to change long-established habits.

Higher Education

According to LEED statistics, higher education projects make up 7 percent, or slightly more than 150, of the first 2,200 LEED-registered projects through September 30, 2005.

College housing is a large and growing market, with the explosion of college registrations since 2000 expected to last through 2009, so a significant number of LEED projects in higher education will involve student housing, research labs and general office/classroom facilities. The market for higher education projects also includes such facilities as libraries, performing arts centers, recreation and athletic facilities, student centers and combinations of these facilities. In the campus environment, at least 50 percent of LEED projects exist due to strong support from the institution's top leadership.[11]

One project in construction at Humboldt State University in Arcata, California, is a 90,000-square-foot classroom and office building, with a contractor-led project development team aiming to achieve a Gold level. This California State University system project based about 15 percent of the total project evaluation on energy conservation and green design measures. The team guaranteed achieving LEED Gold certification as part of its proposal, using daylighting, natural ventilation, high levels of energy conservation, 100 percent rainwater capture and recycling, and considerable use of recycled-content and low-VOC building materials. This project is expected to be the first LEED Gold certified building in the 23-campus California State University system. (The University of California system and the dozens of local community college districts in California run separate systems and have begun to include more green building requirements in their design and construction programs.)

The important role played by various stakeholders makes the college and university market markedly different from the K-12 education market. In higher education, students and faculty are far more influential, with sustainability being a major buzzword on campus. As a result, green buildings are starting to acquire momentum as a force in new construction design. These buildings also offer many opportunities to incorporate green buildings into the curriculum, involving multiple departments such as environmental studies, architecture and engineering. There is considerable faculty interest in getting sustainability issues and considerations into coursework and research.[12] Some university administrators are also beginning to see opportunities for green building programs to assist with fundraising and with student and faculty recruitment.[13]

In spring 2004, the author conducted a Web-based survey of more than 1,000 college and campus planners, architects and facilities directors. When asked whether projects had sustainability goals, 89 percent of the respondents said yes. The goals ranged from green goals in the building program, to green purchasing policies, specific LEED goals and tie-ins to specific campus programs such as composting and recycling. Energy conservation and recycling were key factors in nearly 90 percent of the projects. Half of the respondents had campuses with coursework in sustainability, and nearly half had specific LEED goals, formal mission statements about sustainability and some type of sustainability committee.

From a marketing point of view, 80 percent of the survey respondents identified the facilities director and department (along with a campus architect who is frequently situated in that area) as instrumental in these programs and goals, with 60 percent identifying top-level administrators, 59 percent students and 54 percent faculty. This survey clearly shows the role of key stakeholders from the faculty, students and staff in influencing decisions to go green at the campus level. Interestingly, 50 percent of respondents said that top-level support was strong or fairly strong for their green building programs. Top-level support was strongest at the smaller public and private institutions, where one might expect the chancellor, president or provost to be more actively involved in all aspects of campus life.

Energy issues — such as daylighting, energy conservation goals and use of renewable energy — are quite important in these projects, as are recycling construction and demolition debris and using recycled-content materials. LEED certification is a goal for a majority of the projects. In terms of design process, 52 percent reported conducting a design charrette or sustainability forum as part of a green building project.

This group of buyers and owners cited certain barriers to implementation of green design goals, practices and technologies in their building projects. Most respondents (87 percent) cited increased costs, whether real or perceived, as a barrier; 31 percent said the project was not seen as an administration priority; 23 percent cited the lack of experience with green design; and 18 percent mentioned the lack of a strong campus constituency. Other barriers cited included high soft costs for LEED documentation and required services, local building codes, project schedules and other time constraints; difficulty of integrating capital and operating budgets to justify the higher initial cost of energy conservation investments with future savings; and poor timing of introducing green goals or sustainability values into a project.

When asked what would increase their comfort level with green building goals, processes and technologies, 61 percent of the respondents wanted cost information in standard formats such as RSMeans,[14] while 58 percent wanted standardized cost information on specific green building elements, such as green roofs, photovoltaics and energy efficiency measures. Nearly half (46 percent) cited the need for more of their own experience to feel comfortable, while more than 40 percent wanted to see detailed case studies of university projects and/or local green building projects they could learn from. More than a third wanted specific information on the cost of LEED projects, particularly at various levels of certification.

The market for green buildings for public agencies is perhaps the largest single green market in the U.S., and it is growing rapidly. The combined office, public safety and recreation segments exceed $43 billion per year, much of it in smaller buildings. Whether for office buildings, public safety and order, cultural or recreational projects or public housing, there is a rising demand to meet the increasing array of public policy pronouncements in favor of achieving LEED certification for all new building projects.

Public Facilities Other than Offices

As a final guide to marketers, the survey respondents were asked to comment on how they would approach sustainability in future projects. Several suggested that they would add sustainability to campus planning as a guiding principle and that they would add sustainable design criteria to the overall design guidance. (In fact, we see increasing evidence that there are active sustainability task forces at most major universities.)[15] The main difficulty cited in their comments about investments in energy efficiency, for example, was the separation between capital and operating budgets and the difficulty of getting additional capital appropriations for improvements that go much beyond code.

Types of public agency projects with LEED goals often include:

- police stations and emergency communications centers
- fire stations
- swimming pools and recreation centers
- community centers and senior centers
- museums, libraries and visitor centers
- performing arts centers
- city halls and county administrative centers
- convention centers
- office buildings of all kinds
- airports
- courthouses and jails
- warehouses and vehicle maintenance facilities
- public housing

case study

Living Green Along the Hudson

New York City: The Solaire

New York City's Battery Park City Authority developed the Solaire, a 27-story, 357,000-square-foot apartment building that received extensive publicity and rented its 293 units in five minutes, at 4 to 5 percent above local market rates.[18] Developed for the Authority by the Albanese Organization, the Solaire (www.thesolaire.com) features extensive use of solar photovoltaic (PV) panels and estimates it will cut overall energy use by 35 percent and peak-period electricity use by 65 percent, a major savings in a very high-energy-price city. The Solaire received a LEED Gold rating in 2003 and also a Top Ten award from the Committee on the Environment of the American Institute of Architects (www.aiatopten.org).

The project features an on-site wastewater treatment system, stormwater catchments to irrigate a rooftop garden on the 19th floor, upgraded residential air filtering and a PV system that supplies 5 percent of the building's peak electric power demand. Each year, 5,000 gallons of treated wastewater are used for landscape irrigation. Marketing for the Solaire included extensive local publicity around the groundbreaking in 2001 and heavy use of a Web site, including a construction webcam during the development. The Web site makes frequent mention of the green features, including a focus on healthy indoor air, certainly a major concern in New York City.

Tax credits and state grants totaled $3.3 million for this $115 million project, built for a construction cost of $247 per square foot and completed in August 2003.[19] This project has a breathtaking location along the Hudson River, with views to New Jersey and New York Harbor, including the Statue of Liberty, and a riverfront public park adjacent to the building, making it a highly unusual example of green marketing.

Federal projects tend to be the largest, followed by state government buildings (Table 2.2). The U.S. General Services Administration has been one of the leaders in adopting LEED and pushing it into their projects through the Design Excellence Program. The federal budgeting process also seems conducive to using green building measures, since the government is a long-term owner-operator and has a long-standing commitment to energy conservation in buildings through the Federal Energy Management Program.[16]

Housing

As a vertical market for green buildings, housing is just starting to develop. Multiunit (above three stories) residential LEED registrations are running at about 3 percent of the total, or just under 70 of the initial 2,200 registrations through September 2005. The first LEED-Gold high-rise apartment project, The Solaire in New York City, was certified at the end of 2003. A second project, The Henry, a 15-story condominium project in Portland, Oregon, was certified at LEED Silver in 2004. A 16-story apartment building in Portland, The Louisa, has submitted documentation for LEED Gold, which it expects in 2006.[17]

Based on September 2005 USGBC data, LEED has certified only four other private-sector housing projects, both at the basic (Certified) level, and about eight student residences on campuses, so this segment of the market is still early in the development or innovator stage.

Stephen E. Epler Hall at Portland State University, completed in 2003, is a LEED Silver project with 123 residential units on five floors. The project is 35 percent more energy-efficient than local code, recycles 26 percent of its rainwater for flushing toilets in the first-floor public use area and provides extensive daylighting. It received its LEED certification in October 2004. Projects such as Epler Hall are becoming increasingly common on campuses. This suggests that student housing is an emerging market for green building, particularly developer-led projects. Such projects offer a way to attract students and promote the university's commitment to sustainability. There are a number of nonprofit (and for-profit) organizations in this marketplace that may make good teaming partners for developers, since they can operate the project after it is built.

ENDNOTES

1. See www.lohas.com for a description of this growing market.

2. Green Building Smart Market Report, McGraw-Hill Construction, November 2005, p. 12; available from www.construction.com/SmartMarket/greenbuilding/default.asp.

3. USGBC, as of September 2005.

4. USGBC Member Update, September 2005.

5. The first year of data is for 2000, and the sixth year is for 2005 (projected year-end). Observe the congruence of the growth curves, including LEED registrations (x 10 percent) and total LEED project area, in millions of gross square feet. However, note that LEED project certifications are now growing faster than new project registrations, partly as they catch up to the surge of registrations in 2003, 2004 and 2005.

6.   Survey results are available at www.zoomerang.com/reports/public_report.zgi?ID=L223FGQFK35J

7.   Environmental Design + Construction, Dec. 1, 2004; available at www.edcmag.org.

8.   Data in this section are taken primarily from the U.S. Department of Energy's High-Performance Buildings Database, available at www.eere.energy.gov/buildings/database, as well as the author's personal knowledge.

9.   U.S. Census Bureau, "Monthly Construction Starts," available at www.census.gov/const/C30/release.pdf.

10.   Available at www.turnerconstruction.com/greensurvey05.pdf.

11.   Higher education green building survey conducted by the author, March 2004.

12.   See, for example, the Association for the Advancement of Sustainability in Higher Education (www.aashe.org) and Engineers for a Sustainable World (www.esustainableworld.org).

13.   See, for example, Campus Sustainability and Green Building, Environmental Studies Department, Lewis and Clark College, Portland, Oregon, www.lclark.edu/dept/esm/green_building.html.

14.   www.rsmeans.com/costdata/index.asp.

15.   A good example is the Office of Sustainability Initiatives at Arizona State University in Tempe, www.asu.edu/sustainability.

16.   www.eere.energy.gov/femp/.

17.   Scott Lewis, Brightworks Northwest, personal communication.

18.   For more about the Solaire, see *USA Today*, March 31, 2004; *Urban Land*, February 2005, p. 61; and www.batteryparkcity.org.

19.   See http://leedcasestudies.usgbc.org.

The Plaza at PPL Center, Allentown, Pennsylvania, developed by Liberty Property Trust.
Photography by Peter Aaron-Esto.

BUILDING GREEN FEATURES
INTO YOUR PROJECTS

Creating green buildings requires an integrated design and building process in which all key players work together from the beginning.

Developers and owners have realized cost savings of 1 to 3 percent in design and construction with integrated design approaches and other nontraditional measures, such as involving the general contractor and key subcontractors earlier in the process to help with pricing alternative approaches to achieve required performance levels.[1]

The traditional linear design-bid-build process can work against the development of green buildings. The sequential handoff from architect to engineers to contractor involves little feedback, so that the engineering aspects of building operating costs and comfort considerations may not be related back to basic building design features. As a result, key design decisions are often made without considering long-term operations. The mechanical engineer, for example, is often insulated from the architect's building envelope design considerations, yet that set of decisions can be critical in determining the size and cost of the HVAC plant, which can often consume up to 20 percent of a building's cost. The traditional value engineering exercise, usually conducted after the project is clearly over budget, often involves reducing the value of the HVAC systems by specifying lower-efficiency (cheaper) equipment and possibly reducing the R-value of glazing and insulation — measures that will reduce first costs but lead to higher lifetime operating costs, which typically account for 80 percent or more of a building's total costs.

Who Is Involved

Many professional disciplines have roles to play in a typical building project:

- *Architects* naturally have the task of coordinating overall building design and dealing directly with such issues as the building envelope, daylighting, materials selection, and window and roof specifications.

Getting Started in Green Development

How should a developer new to green buildings tackle its first project? Successful green developers offer these suggestions:

- Target a specific market segment amenable to green building, including major corporate real estate, government buildings, colleges and universities and high-rise housing.

- Find a location where the knowledge workers are in greater abundance (the group Richard Florida calls the Creative Class), since it is likely you will be more successful there.

- Hire a design team experienced in green buildings, accomplished at incorporating sustainable design elements and with a good record in project cost management

- Hire a contractor-project manager with a strong interest in green building and a good track record with prior projects.

- Make sure your own corporate values align with sustainability objectives of green buildings. Consistent values will give you the resilience to overcome some of the hurdles in the process.

- Look to reduce risk by maximizing utility and other incentive payments, taking advantage of accelerated local government permit processes and other support measures that favor green buildings.

- Hire a good PR and marketing agency from the beginning, to help brand the project, the approach and the development firm itself.

- Insist on high-performance results from the design and construction team on a conventional budget.

- Set specific goals for LEED attainment, such as LEED Silver certification.

- Take a LEED workshop or employ an experienced LEED project consultant to guide you through the process.

- Employ an integrated design approach that begins with an early-stage eco-charrette and continues throughout the design and construction process, including value engineering reviews.

- Bring the contractor on board early for pricing and general feedback on approaches recommended by the design team.

- Make sure all major subcontractors are on board with the green emphasis of the project.

- *Interior designers* deal with materials selection for furniture and furnishings and help specify low-VOC paints, carpets and similar low-toxicity items. They may also be asked to assist with specifying elements of under-floor air distribution systems, such as carpet tile.

- *Mechanical and electrical engineers* can contribute between 25 and 50 percent of the total points required for LEED certification, focusing on water conservation, rainwater reclamation and gray water reuse systems, energy efficiency, lighting design, commissioning, indoor air quality, carbon dioxide monitoring and thermal comfort.

- *Energy engineers* are called upon to prepare energy models for buildings and to design onsite power systems such as microturbines and combined heat and power (CHP) plants.

- *Civil engineers* have to deal with stormwater management, provide input on rainwater reclamation systems, prepare erosion and sedimentation control plans, and sometimes advise on constructed wetlands, bioswales and onsite waste treatment systems.

- *Landscape architects* need to consider water efficiency of landscaping design, assist with design of detention ponds, bioswales and constructed wetlands, and also oversee site restoration programs.

- *Structural engineers* are asked to consider the relative benefits of wood, steel and concrete in structural systems, given their different effects on sustainable design. Often projects that use passive thermal conditioning require heavy mass structural components such as concrete. Structural engineers also have a role to play in green roof technology.

- *Cost consultants* have a significant role to play in assessing the costs of innovative green building systems, such as eco-roofs, solar power, and stormwater retention systems, as well as advising clients on the overall costs of green buildings.

- *General contractors* have to provide for recycling of construction debris (often at a 90 percent or better level) and of documenting the costs of all of the materials that go into a building. They oversee the construction indoor air quality management plans and activities, and they play a vital role in documenting the costs of the project. Contractors are also responsible for LEED credits relating to construction staging, indoor air quality management and erosion control plans.

- *Subcontractors* are often asked to work with unfamiliar or hard-to-obtain recycled-content materials and to document the costs they incur. Mechanical and electrical subcontractors often have to interact with the building commissioning process as well.

- *Environmental consulting firms* also have a role to play in sustainable site selection practices and assessment of the potential for on-site stormwater management, brownfield redevelopment and site restoration, for example.

Charrette-Based Design

The integrated approach often involves intensive design exercises, called eco-charrettes, with key stakeholders during programming or conceptual design and with key design team members at the outset of schematic design. Charrettes are a quick and economical way to invite input and explore design options as a group before settling on a preferred direction. During a charrette the owner or developer hears competing approaches to meeting program requirements and can be a more informed participant in the design process.[2] A refinement of the charrette involves day-long goal-setting sessions with the owner or developer and key stakeholders early in the design process. These sessions clarify guidance to design teams about preferred sustainability measures and can assist in making budget-driven tradeoffs later in design.

Integrated design requires considerably more upfront effort before the schematic design phase, including dialogue, charrettes, studies and timely decisionmaking. It also requires additional fees to architects and engineers. On small projects, these fees might add 1 to 2 percent to the total project cost; for a $5 million project, for example, $50,000 would provide for a full charrette-based design process with energy and daylight modeling studies. The investment can yield a more efficient design process and more effective building performance.

A MIXTURE OF STRATEGIES

The developer who wants to build green features into a project chooses different principles and technologies to form a strategy for sustainable development. A project can incorporate a few or many of these principles, which can be grouped in five areas:

- Sustainable sites — Location that reduces sprawl and preserves natural land; building orientation and shape that maximize solar heat gain and daylighting; landscaping and green roofs to absorb heat and provide insulation; stormwater management techniques that reduce pollution runoff.

case study

Keeping Employees Healthy and Happy

Pittsburgh: PNC Firstside Center

This five-story, 647,000-square-foot office building opened in 2000 and was the first LEED-NC Silver certified project in the United States. It was developed on a brownfield site for PNC Financial Services Group. Typically, 1,800 employees occupy the building 24 hours a day, 7 days a week. Total project cost, excluding land, was $108 million, or about $154 per square foot. Annual energy use (measured) is about 29 kwh per square foot, or about $2.90 per square foot at 10 cents per kwh. Higher energy consumption is explained largely by the round-the-clock operations.

In deciding on energy-efficiency investments, PNC used a strict two-year payback criterion. The project employed an innovative approach to HVAC, using ventilation air distributed beneath the raised floor with local diffusers that occupants can control. This system lets each employee adjust diffusers in the floor of each workstation for individual comfort. Overhead variable-air-volume (VAV) units recirculate conditioned air for local needs and for more simplistic control. A building automation system monitors and regulates temperature, humidity and carbon dioxide concentrations. However, the real surprise is the positive impact of daylighting, healthy indoor air and other green building features on worker productivity and on retention of key employees.[3]

- Water efficiency — Landscaping that requires minimal irrigation; fixtures that reduce water consumption or use recycled water; cooling towers that conserve water by using recycled rainwater.

- Energy and atmosphere — High-efficiency windows, daylight design elements, efficient lighting design, HVAC systems and office equipment that reduce electricity consumption.

- Materials and resources — Reused and recycled materials that save money and conserve natural resources; use of sustainably harvested wood and specification of rapidly renewable materials such as wheatboard cabinetry.

- Indoor environmental quality — Low-toxicity materials and furnishings, limited use of harmful cleaning solvents and well-ventilated spaces that protect building occupants.

A review of green building products and design measures used in LEED-certified projects illustrates the range of possibilities for building green features into a project (Tables 3.1, 3.2). The list includes three categories: highly likely, somewhat likely and less often used. As the market for higher levels of LEED certification grows, products in the "somewhat likely" category, such as CO_2 monitors, may become "highly likely." Other products, such as photovoltaics and FSC-certified wood, will move into the "somewhat likely" category because they are visible signs of commitment to sustainable building. Based on this information, Table 3.3 shows the estimated market size for various green building measures for a year in which 1,000 projects register for LEED certification. (Registrations reached this level in 2005.)

Many other measures that receive LEED points involve design and construction decisions that are made at various stages of the integrated design and building process, including specifications and other construction documents. These decisions are more likely to be influenced by the project's LEED goals, by the use of an integrated design process and by the relative green design skills of the firms involved.

Even in this brief rendition, it is clear that identifiable green measures in LEED-registered buildings may account for nearly $800 million in new market value in 2006. Adding in the large expenditures for energy efficiency measures with relatively quick paybacks, billions of additional dollars may be spent on green materials and systems — much of it replacing expenditures on less green items — stemming from projects' decisions to increase their level of sustainability.

Table 3.1
Green Measures Used in LEED-Certified Projects

Highly likely to be used (67 percent or more of projects)

- Low-VOC paints, coatings, adhesives, sealants

- Low-VOC carpeting

- 10 percent or more recycled-content materials

- Views to the outdoors from 90 percent of spaces

- Two innovation credits, such as public education or high levels of construction waste recycling

Somewhat likely to be used (33 to 66 percent of projects)

- Two-week building flush-out before occupancy

- Carbon-dioxide monitors to improve ventilation effectiveness

- Bioswales, detention/retention ponds and rainwater reclamation systems

- Green roofs or Energy Star® roofs

- Construction-period indoor air quality maintenance

- Permanent temperature and humidity monitoring systems

- Daylighting for at least 75 percent of spaces

- Cutoff light fixtures and lower outdoor ambient lighting levels

- Water-conserving fixtures and waterless urinals (30% reduction in 54 percent of projects)

- At least a 35 percent energy use reduction over baseline levels (based on ASHRAE 90.1–1999)

- Additional building commissioning: peer review of design-phase documents

- Purchased green power for at least two years

- No added urea-formaldehyde (UF) in composite wood or agrifiber products

Less often used (less than 33 percent of projects)

- Solar photovoltaics (9 to 13 percent)

- Electric vehicle charging stations/alternative-fuel vehicles (31 percent)

- Measurement and verification systems using U.S. Dept. of Energy protocols (30 percent)

- Site restoration with native plants (29 percent)

- Use of FSC-certified wood products (26 percent)

- High-efficiency ventilation, including under-floor air systems (25 percent)

- Operable windows (30 percent)

- Rapidly renewable materials, such as cork, bamboo, agrifiber boards and linoleum products (6 percent)

Source: USGBC, analysis of scorecards from the first 195 LEED-NC v.2.0/2.1 certified projects, June 2005; available at www.usgbc.org. Courtesy of Paul Shariari, Green Light Strategies, www.greenlightstrategies.com

Table 3.2
Specific LEED Points Used in LEED-Certified Projects
(arranged by order of LEED credits)

LEED Credit Category	% of Projects Certifying	Typical Measures
SS 4.3 Alternative fuels	31	Electric vehicle charging, hybrids
SS 5.2 Site restoration	58	Preserve habitat, use native plants
SS 6.1 Stormwater management	37	Bioswales, detention ponds, rainwater capture and recycling
SS 7.2 Urban heat island effect	46	Green (vegetated) roofs, Energy Star roofs with high emissivity
SS 8 Light pollution reduction	46	Cutoff fixtures, lower night lighting
WE 3.2 30% Water use reduction	54	Low-use fixtures, waterless urinals
EA 1.1 to 1.5 Project achieved 35% reduction vs. ASHRAE 90.1-1999	42	High-performance glazing, reduced lighting levels, better envelope
EA 2.2 10% renewables	9	Photovoltaics, on-site renewables
EA 3 Additional commissioning	47	Third-party commissioning
EA 5 Measurement/verification	30	Additional energy monitoring
EA 6 Purchased green power	36	Buy green power for two years
MR 4.2 10% Recycled content materials	67	Specify recycled-content materials
MR 6 Rapidly renewable materials	6	Cork, linoleum, agrifiber MDF
MR 7 50% of wood products certified	26	FSC-certified lumber
EQ 1 Carbon dioxide monitors	55	CO_2 monitors
EQ 2 High-efficiency ventilation	25	Under-floor air systems
EQ 3.1 Construction indoor air quality	54	Best practices/MERV-13 filters
EQ 3.2 Air quality prior to occupancy	56	Two-week flush-out
EQ 4.1/4.2 Low-VOC paints/adhesives	80	Specify low-VOC materials
EQ 4.3 Low-emission carpeting	93	Specify low-VOC carpeting
EQ 4.4 No added UF in composite wood	41	No added UF in composites
EQ 6.1 Thermal comfort at perimeter	30	Operable windows
EQ 6.2 Thermal comfort interior	20	Under-floor air systems
EQ 7.2 Temperature and humidity monitoring	60	Humidification/dehumidification
EQ 8.1 Daylighting for 75% of spaces	39	Light shelves, skylights
EQ 8.2 Views to outdoors	68	Space layout, larger windows

Source: USGBC, analysis of scorecards from the first 195 LEED-NC v.2.0/2.1 certified projects, June 2005; available at www.usgbc.org. Courtesy of Paul Shariari, Green Light Strategies, www.greenlightstrategies.com

Table 3.3
Estimated Minimum Annual Market for Green Building Measures in LEED-Registered Projects
(ordered by market value)

Green Building Measure	% of Projects Using Measure (100 projects)	% of Total Materials Cost	Estimated Market Value in 2006 (1,000 projects)
Recycled content	67%	10%[a]	$377 million
Low-VOC carpet	93%	NA	$150 million[b]
Under-floor air systems	20%	N/A	$ 120 million[c]
Photovoltaic systems	9%	N/A[d]	$ 72 million[e]
Certified wood	26%	1%[f]	$ 29 million[g]
Low-VOC paints, sealants, adhesives, etc.	80%	0.5% (est.)	$ 22 million
Rapidly renewable materials	6%	5%	$ 17 million
Green roofs	10%	N/A	$ 15 million[h]
Waterless urinals	40%[i]	N/A	$ 2 million

Assumptions: 1,000 LEED registrations, average project size 100,000 square feet, project construction cost $125 per square foot, materials cost at 45 percent of construction cost (default value in the LEED calculator), giving an estimate of total materials cost at $5.63 billion for LEED projects.

Note: ss= sustainable sites; we = water efficiency; ea = energy and atmosphere; mr = materials and resources; eq = indoor environmental quality.

[a] Recycled content at 10 percent of total materials cost achieves two LEED points in materials and resources.

[b] Not included in total project materials cost; same for green roofs and under-floor air systems.

[c] Estimated at 200 projects, 100,000 square feet per project, $6 per square foot premium cost for flooring system and diffusers; does not include carpet tile or other approaches to UF air systems.

[d] Based on carpeting at $1.50 per square foot, 100,000 sq. ft. per project, 1,000 projects. Total market for low-VOC carpet is probably much greater.

[e] Estimated at 10 mw total, $8 million/mw installed price (total U.S. commercial/industrial installations in 2005 are likely to exceed 60 mw (source: Paul Maycock, publisher, *PV News*, personal communication).

[f] For certified wood, assume 4 percent of total materials cost is wood and 50 percent is certified wood.

[g] According to industry insiders, the total market for recycled wood products is much larger, probably exceeding $400 million per year, most of it sold in home improvement centers.

[h] Estimated at 10,000 square feet per system (20,000 square feet average floor plate), $15 per square foot incremental cost, or $150,000 per installation. Based on 53 percent of projects choosing a green roof at 50 percent coverage, or an Energy Star/high-emissivity roof at 75 percent coverage, and green roofs representing about 20 percent of the total.

[i] Estimate based on 53 percent of projects achieving 30 percent water use reduction inside the building and about 80 percent of those using 10 waterless urinals per building at a cost of $5,000.

WHAT MAKES A GREEN DEVELOPMENT SUCCESSFUL?

There is no single factor that makes a development green or makes it successful. What matters is each developer's intention to make a strong green building statement and the design team's successful execution of the project. Successful green developments share some common characteristics:

- **Location.** Experienced developers pay attention to the first axiom of real estate: location trumps everything. Most successful projects are located in urban core areas or in areas with key tenants already in place. Many successful green commercial office developments are occurring in the cities and metropolitan areas where knowledge workers reside and work, including Boston, New York, Chicago, Atlanta, Seattle, Portland (Oregon) and Washington, D.C.

- **Price.** Most green commercial office buildings are built and leased, rented or sold at market rates. Many are large enough to accommodate some additional initial investment costs for energy-saving improvements and for LEED-related documentation. However, even the smaller developments seem able to accommodate extra costs in order to meet larger marketing and sustainable development goals. Still, building green on a conventional budget remains a key goal for most developers.

- **Market segments targeted.** Commercial offices are by far the easiest segments to target, since this building type has a broad demand profile and since the LEED-NC system was designed with offices in mind. However, there are also successful green developments of laboratories and corporate headquarters, including build-to-suit projects.

- **Attention to design and corporate values.** Most successful green developments are for Class-A office space in which design quality, urban amenities and building features are important to tenants and these tenants are sophisticated buyers of such space. It is easier to explain green building values in a property to tenants who have done their homework and who understand the productivity and related benefits of green building features. In addition, corporate values play a critical role in developing green buildings. It is more than

case study

Location, Location

Washington, D.C.: National Association of REALTORS® Headquarters

Built on a brownfield site (an abandoned gas station) and a derelict park, this 95,000-square-foot, 12-story, owner-developed building received a LEED-NC Silver rating upon opening in September 2005. Energy savings are estimated at $56,000 per year, or about 60 cents per square foot. About 90 percent of habitable spaces have daylighting and direct views of the outdoors. Cost of the building was $46 million, including site remediation. The realtors' group occupies about 40,000 square feet on five floors, with seven floors available to other tenants.

a simple business decision about minimizing the per-square-foot cost. Liberty REIT, for example, sought to develop better-value buildings and potentially attract new investors from the socially responsible investing space. Hines, a leading build-and-hold developer, wants buildings with lower operating costs and better tenants, but also believes in being responsible with investors' money. Gerding/Edlen Development in Portland responds to its tenants' and buyers' interest in sustainable buildings in the company's core market area and promotes its own corporate values related to sustainable development. (See the Case Studies CD for information on how the Arizona Department of Environmental Quality demonstrated its mission through construction of a new LEED-certified headquarters, developed by Opus West.)

- **Branding and differentiation.** Every real estate market is tough in that there are always significant competitors. The ability to get media exposure from green buildings is an attractive feature and is often a key element of the marketing program. A green building helps the developer differentiate its property from other similar buildings in the same submarket and attract core tenants from knowledge-based professional service firms.

- **Timing.** Most commercially successful speculative green buildings have come on line since 2001, when the economy began to recover from recession and the overbuilding of office space to accommodate the dot-com era of the late 1990s. Progressive developers in all parts of the country are getting involved in green buildings to gain experience with these new techniques and technologies. Developers also do not want to be left with less valuable properties five or more years from now, when the first round of leases come up for renewal and they have to compete with nearby buildings that are LEED-certified and therefore more attractive to prospective tenants.

ENDNOTES

1.   See for example, "Platinum on a Budget," *Consulting-Specifying Engineer*, October 2005, www.csemag.com/article/CA6271678.html?text=Platinum.

2.   For a good description of how this dialogue might work, see articles by architect and LEED co-developer William Reed on integrated design and regenerative design at www.natlogic.com/Articles/Bill-Reed_Questions.pdf.

3.   Gary Saulson, senior vice president, facilities, PNC, personal communication.

Atlantic Station, Atlanta, Georgia, developed by AIG Global Real Estate Investment Corp. and Jacoby Development.

POSITIONING YOUR COMPANY AS A GREEN DEVELOPER

Sustainability is not a destination, but a journey. By making a strong corporate commitment to sustainable design and operations, many developers are beginning to walk the talk in an open way. Cities and investors appreciate working with developers who share their values and are willing to experiment with new technologies and processes. This is true contemporary marketing: building relationships based on shared values.

To approach the green building market, it is useful to think of it in terms of technological innovation. Marketing history tells us that most innovations take considerable time to reach the marketplace. Typically, it takes a generation — 15 to 25 years — for more than 90 percent of the market to adopt an innovation. The innovation typically must have a major cost or business advantage over existing methods — greater than 25 percent, if cost alone is the criterion. This cost-effectiveness barrier exists because of the costs of learning new methods, the economic risk of investing capital to create new things and the business risk inherent in trying something new. Because the building industry historically has resisted discontinuous innovation, buildings are built much the same as they were 20 years ago, relying on incremental innovations to improve performance.

Of course, many technical and technological innovations never achieve mainstream status, often owing to cost or complexity. Think, for example, of all the PDA products developed before the Palm Pilot™ finally captured the mainstream business market. To the degree that green buildings are simply higher-performing buildings, one can argue that there's not much new and that designing and building better buildings can readily be accomplished by the existing industry. However, if the innovation is rating and certifying buildings against energy and environmental design criteria, as in the LEED green building rating system, then the classical theory of diffusion of innovations can be applied to forecast market demand. This theory explains the substitution of new ways of doing things for old ways, in a predictable pattern. Given the large numbers of people now trained in the LEED system (more than 23,000 LEED Accredited Professionals, and about 29,000 who have attended the LEED training workshop), one can argue that LEED has all the hallmarks of a self-sustaining innovation. Therefore, its adoption rate can be predicted by using diffusion of innovations theory.

The theory of diffusion of innovations gives powerful insight into customer behavior. Only about 3 percent of clients are likely to be *innovators* and willing to pursue a new design trend or technology development before seeing how others have done with it. Another 13 percent or so are *early adopters* who are likely following these trends and developments closely and are willing to try them once they see a few successful experiments or case studies. The remaining population of clients — the *early majority, late majority and laggards* — generally will not embrace change or take risk without clear evidence of benefit and a clear record of accomplishment to examine. They are the "wait and see" crowd and, at this time, generally represent a waste of time for marketers.

This analysis suggests that developers need to be selective about which clients and funding sources they pursue for green building projects and how they approach them, with which aspect of the business case. Your past successful (and documented) experience will be a powerful selling point in convincing clients and investors to pursue LEED-registered projects with you.

In addition, developers should research what innovations a client has embraced in the past, what internal and external forces are driving them to consider green design and in which areas of technology and operations the client is likely to have greater tolerance for risk and ambiguity.

Positioning your company as a green developer requires making a visible commitment to sustainable design and development. How should marketers advise their firms to take advantage of green market opportunities? Here are some of the methods various firms have found successful:

- An in-house "Green Team" that offers internal consulting to projects.

- Internal training and education, including staff-led and vendor-led in-house sessions and support for attending conferences and outside training.

- Management of green building information, including a library and development of in-house specifications for green projects.

- Availability of tools, including energy modeling software and metrics for determining shades of green, such as LEED. For a developer, understanding the costs and limits of such tools is important to managing a design team's activities and costs.

- Use of outside expertise or capable subconsultants, such as mechanical, electrical and civil engineers.

- Goals set for green projects, including LEED for client projects and internal assessments using LEED for all projects. Some firms start every project with the intent to green it as much as possible, regardless of budget or expressed marketplace interest.[1]

A cautionary word: not every project is a candidate for green marketing. Not every client wants to be the first kid on the block to have a new toy or to be a technology leader. While some developers trust their architects and are willing to follow their lead in pursuing a green building agenda (especially true, in the author's experience, for higher education projects), most corporate and building owners are more cautious, and speculative developers, for the most part, are still in the "wait and see" stage.

This chapter describes seven steps to successful positioning:

1. Provide internal education opportunities.
2. Make sustainable improvements in operations.
3. Implement a green communications strategy.
4. Build a strong green-development presence in the marketplace.
5. Differentiate your company.
6. Build internal capabilities.
7. Integrate green design and marketing activities.

INTERNAL EDUCATION

Interface Engineering, a five-office, 125-person firm based in Portland, Oregon, promotes sustainability through a variety of education-related activities that developers can emulate. By putting well-trained, knowledgeable people on project teams, the firm complements its normal continuing education in energy engineering, lighting design, plumbing engineering and related topics with a strong in-house training program in the LEED green building rating system. The firm has begun training its corporate staff in the Natural Step™ system (www.ortns.org) and uses Honda Civic hybrid cars for project travel to reduce gasoline use.

case study

An Integrated Green Commitment

Dallas: Turner Construction

Turner Construction is the largest commercial construction firm in the United States, with annual revenues of more than $6 billion in 2002 and more than $7 billion in 2004.[2] In September 2004, Turner's CEO Tom Leppert announced a formal commitment to sustainable construction and business practices as a means to continue strengthening Turner's leadership position.[3] Leppert asserted that Turner's plan to be "the [leading] responsible builder is good for the environment, and also for building owners, developers and occupants." Equally important, he stated that these practices are good for the bottom line and serve as an example to the entire construction industry. As the largest firm in the industry, Turner has effectively thrown down the gauntlet for other major construction firms. This development is extremely important for the growth of the green building industry, since most sophisticated building owners and developers rely heavily on the advice of their builders in deciding to adopt green building design for their projects.

Leppert states: "As our experience in green building has grown we've learned that costs, contrary to common belief, can be contained to a level comparable to traditional, non-sustainable buildings and generate additional, important benefits for our clients and our local communities. Turner plans to leverage this experience and increase its already-broad involvement with green practices for the advantage of our employees, our clients and the environment."

The Turner green program consists of:

- Mandating construction waste recycling on all Turner projects, not just green design projects. Recycling efforts will be phased in until Turner reaches a 100 percent waste diversion goal.

- Ensuring that over time, all Turner field offices will be green-friendly. In these buildings, Turner will incorporate field waste recycling programs, energy-efficient lighting on timers, operable windows for natural ventilation and water-efficient fixtures.

- Implementing a collaborative sponsorship with the USGBC of the Emerging Green Builders program to help improve sustainable building curriculums at colleges and to recognize those students who will promote future green building growth.

- Instituting a major green training program for Turner employees. The online Turner Knowledge Network will help employees learn about the LEED standard to add to their knowledge of green field operations guidelines. This training role is critical to the marketing of the green capability and is often overlooked, especially in the construction field.

- Doubling the number of Turner's LEED Accredited Professionals from 42 to 84 by the end of the first year. While this is not a large number, it is a beginning.[4]

- Creating an advisory council of outside industry experts to provide objective advice on sustainable design best practices and to drive their adoption with the company and its clients.

- Naming a senior vice president, Rod Wille, to lead Turner's Center of Excellence, which links Turner's local and national green information. Wille has been in this role informally and his inside knowledge and credibility have materially advanced green building initiatives.

case study

One Turner project, Genzyme Center in Cambridge, Massachusetts (described on the case studies CD), received a LEED Platinum rating in 2005. Within Genzyme's budget, Turner was able to incorporate innovative features, including sun-tracking mirrors to direct daylight into the building, natural ventilation using the atrium, and a double-skin exterior wall and extensive indoor gardens for the enjoyment of occupants and to improve indoor air quality. During procurement, Turner helped Genzyme and the design team ensure that the contract documents incorporated the green elements Genzyme wanted and that subcontract bidders used cost-effective products and methods to achieve the LEED Platinum rating within the budget constraints.

In 2003, Turner partnered with Toyota to develop a LEED-Gold certified building in Torrance, California, that cost no more than a traditionally constructed building. The Toyota Motor Sales South Campus building is 636,000 square feet on a 38-acre site. For use as administrative offices, it features 53,000 square feet of rooftop photovoltaic panels that can generate 550 kilowatts of electricity, about 20 percent of its total energy usage. Its first cost was competitive with the cost of other local, conventional office buildings.

"The expected increase in green building benefits us all, especially Turner clients," says Leppert. "It streamlines processes and controls upfront costs for construction while ensuring that sustainable methods will be used whenever possible." As of September 2005 , Turner had completed or had under contract more than 130 projects with green building elements, valued at well over $10 billion and totaling more than 40 million square feet. Turner had completed 15 LEED certified projects, with more than 54 additional LEED-registered projects completed or in progress.[5]

Make sure that a large number of your firm's key people become LEED Accredited Professionals (LEED APs). By September 2005, Interface had 25 LEED Accredited Professionals among its technical staff of over 90 people. With more than 23,000 accredited professionals nationwide, there is no longer any excuse for even a smaller developer not to have several on its staff. The USGBC offers public workshops on LEED for New Construction (LEED-NC) nearly 50 times a year, so there's bound to be a training course to which you can send key staff. LEED for Existing Buildings (LEED-EB) and LEED for Commercial Interiors (LEED-CI) workshops are also offered nearly 25 times a year. See www.usgbc.org for a list of workshop locations and dates.

SUSTAINABLE OPERATIONS

Interface Engineering completed a major headquarters move from the suburbs to downtown Portland at the end of 2002. As part of this move, the company was able to increase its own commitment to sustainable building operations, including extensive daylighting and healthier indoor environmental quality. More than 60 percent of the staff now commute by bus, light rail, bicycle or walking; before the move, the number was less than 10 percent. Paper recycling increased after recycling boxes replaced trashcans at employee workstations. The firm has also reduced gas consumption by purchasing Honda Civic hybrid vehicles for its small fleet, and it is passing the savings along to clients.

case study

Positioning for Success

Seattle: Mithun Architects

Mithun CEO Bert Gregory was instrumental in pushing this firm into a focus on sustainable design.[6] The firm grew throughout the 2001 to 2003 national recession (gross service fees increased nearly 30 percent from 2001 to 2003) to about 145 staff members in 2004, including more than 40 LEED APs. It is widely seen as one of the leading green design firms in the Pacific Northwest. Gregory has been with the firm since 1985 and is a leading proponent of sustainable building design and sustainable urban planning.

When asked how the firm took a proactive approach to marketing sustainable design, Gregory responded:

> One proactive element is our commitment to education. It is both internal to the team and external. Many of us speak locally or nationally about topics of sustainability.... Those talks always have intangible but beneficial results in making people aware of our firm.... Proactivity is making sure people are aware of us, making sure that we're establishing relationships and investing in our community.

Sustainability has changed Mithun's practice of design by emphasizing collaborative strategies, using a broad consulting team at the start of a project. Gregory says:

> Such strategies have changed us to be in more of a leadership position on projects that are really complex and need lots of people to do them. More and more projects have an economist or real estate consultant as part of the team.... These days we are spending more time sitting on the same side of the table as our clients, helping them understand the long-term economic impact, return on investment and choices they can make that will establish a higher value for their project or their portfolio. This is really different from how most architects would approach a project.... The distinguishing feature of our practice has been our ability to incorporate design excellence with sustainable strategies.

Gregory believes the future of sustainable design is really at the city level and at the broad-based master planning level. He says, "For individual buildings, the future is in clients and designers establishing goals that are extremely aggressive regarding environmental impact and understanding how we can truly create buildings with limited or no impact."

In terms of competitive posture, Gregory believes: "Ultimately, it [sustainability] is the cost of entry.... For us, research and development is an important aspect of our practice. One way to continue to be a leader is to make sure you are doing R&D. Most strong businesses are including that in their practice."

Mithun has completed several LEED-certified projects and many studies of urban sustainability, including two landmark studies of entire urban districts. *The Resource Guide for Sustainable Development in an Urban Environment*, focusing on the South Lake Union area in Seattle, is a landmark in green neighborhood design and can be downloaded from the Mithun Web site, as can the *2004 Lloyd Crossing Sustainable Urban Master Plan*.

GREEN COMMUNICATIONS STRATEGY

Leading developers know the public relations value of having their people accessible to the media and of building their reputation among their peers as a progressive company. Extending this communications technique to green development lends credibility to a firm's claims of expertise and also provides magazine reprints and other opportunities for marketing this expertise. At Interface Engineering, internal experts publish articles on water conservation, energy engineering and sustainable design in publications for mechanical and electrical engineers, vertical market segments and the local design and construction industry. They speak to a variety of groups, including architects, planners and facility managers, as well as national and international green building conferences.

Tell your story aggressively to as many media outlets as you can. Successful sustainable design projects are still rare enough in many areas of the country and even rarer in specialized market niches (even large market segments, such as K-12 schools, only had eight of the first 106 LEED version 2.0-certified projects).

(See Case Studies on CD for information on how AIG Global Real Estate Investment Corp. garnered publicity from around the globe for its high visibility project, Atlantic Station.)

MARKETPLACE PRESENCE

To build a strong green development presence in the marketplace, it is essential for your principals and key staff to share their knowledge and enthusiasm for sustainable design with potential clients on a regular basis. You will find out what your clients know and want and what your staff does not know and should learn. Provide sustainability studies as an extra service item on all major projects, but be prepared over time to require your consultants to include most of these design services in the base fee, as you learn what is and isn't required for LEED projects.

Explain to your clients why this approach will not only benefit the project directly, but could also result in major marketing benefits for their project, company or organization. The author advocates sharing knowledge in the form of talks, articles, classes, seminars and one-on-one discussions. Leading development firms can successfully differentiate themselves by sharing knowledge with clients and the larger green building community in an appropriate way. This practice often leads to effective marketing through word-of-mouth referrals, improved relationships and team building.

Interface Engineering offers its expertise in public and private seminars to clients such as architects and owners. For several years, the firm has been holding breakfast and lunch seminars in sustainable design for clients and fellow consultants and offering public seminars as part of a group of AIA-approved continuing education courses for architects. Developers might consider holding such events for potential funders, such as pension funds and other socially responsible investors.

Make sure your company joins the U.S. Green Building Council and can use its logo on proposals, stationery and brochures. Joining the USGBC will signal to clients that you have the interest and knowledge they are seeking. The cost will range from a few hundred dollars up to $5,000 a year for fairly large firms. This is probably the best investment a firm can make to establish credibility with clients. Join the local USGBC chapter and become active in it. This provides ideal networking and educational opportunities.

DIFFERENTIATION

To differentiate your company, make sure clients know how your firm will approach the project differently from major competitors by showing your team's design approach and understanding of sustainable design. One North American mechanical engineering firm has shown its commitment to the LEED system, for example, by certifying more than 60 percent of its staff as LEED Accredited Professionals, including some not directly involved in design, and by eagerly embracing and introducing new technologies in its area of expertise. As a result, this firm has established strong roots in new territories with innovative green architects and is well positioned to make further inroads in a wider geographic area. A Portland-based developer has acquired a strong reputation as a green development firm while still building a strong portfolio of commercial opportunities and completed projects.

Know the strengths and weaknesses of the competition in this area of design and construction, so that you'll be prepared to match their strengths and exploit their weaknesses in the proposal and interview stage. You may even decide not to respond to a solicitation from an owner asking for sustainable design, if you think your firm can't yet stand up to the competition for a certain project type or for a client that is already experienced in LEED projects.

INTERNAL CAPABILITIES

Know what the firm's principals and senior-level personnel are doing in the area of sustainable design, and learn what they are hearing about the need for these services among your client base. Incorporate sustainable design requirements into your firm's standard requests for proposal. (Many projects have sustainable design elements that can be used without necessarily being LEED-registered; the author's estimate is that perhaps only 50 percent of the projects with sustainability goals ever register with LEED, owing to cost concerns.) Make sure you're familiar with the language of sustainable design for your design team professionals and, if you're the firm's chief marketer, push the technical types to tell you where your own knowledge base might be a little weak.

Make a major effort to build a portfolio of LEED-registered and LEED-certified projects. Look at your other projects that have sustainability elements and try to incorporate them into your case studies as quickly as possible. Build a library of case studies on successful project experience using sustainable design so that you can market your projects and provide material to the media to help in profiling the firm's expertise.

INTEGRATED GREEN DESIGN AND MARKETING

Once a firm commits to a sustainable building project, the marketing work has just begun, for a successful effort is always the best marketing tool, and one cannot wait for a project to be finished (which might take two to three years) to start generating enthusiastic client support for referrals and testimonials. Early design activity, such as eco-charrettes and green forums, should also have as components a clear presentation of the areas of risk and ambiguity in the project and should develop explicit strategies for dealing with them.

ENDNOTES

1.   *Environmental Building News* 13, no. 5 (May 2004); available at www.buildinggreen.com.

2.   *Building Design & Construction* Annual "Top 300" survey, 2002, available at www.bdcmag.com; Turner Web site, www.turnerconstructioncompany.com.

3.   Turner Construction Company, press release, Sept. 27, 2004, available at www.turnerconstruction.com.

4.   *Building Design & Construction* magazine reported that Turner had 76 LEED APs at the end of June 2005; www.bdcmag.com.

5.   www.turnerconstruction.com/greensurvey05.pdf, p. 26.

6.   Gregory was interviewed in *The Marketer*, April 2004, the monthly magazine of the Society for Marketing Professional Services (www.smps.org). Quotes used by permission of SMPS.

1180 Peachtree, Atlanta, Georgia, developed by Hines. Photography by Greg Mooney, Atlanta Photography.

SEVEN KEYS TO SUCCESSFUL GREEN MARKETING

There is no single competitive response to the growing green building market that is right for every developer, as much has to do with the company's own strategic clarity, capability, capital and character. Nevertheless, a conscious choice among strategies is vastly preferable to having none.

Industry surveys and diffusion of innovations theory (see Chapter 4) contribute to an understanding of what the marketplace for green development wants and needs. Green building developers and organizations that market sustainable design services and projects should incorporate the following information and techniques in their marketing strategies:

- Case study data with solid cost information, including initial cost increases for various green building measures.

- Comparative cost information, within and across building types, as to the full costs of LEED certification, including documentation.

- Demonstrable information and marketplace feedback on the benefits of green buildings beyond well-documented operating cost savings from energy and water conservation. In particular, realization of some of the business-case benefits, such as a rent premium, increased occupancy, faster lease-up and faster permitting, are essential to build credibility for green buildings.

- Clear evidence of demand for green building measures, including realization of the business-case benefits, but also independent studies of consumer and corporate demand, including willingness to pay for specific levels of LEED achievement, as evidenced, for example, by higher rents or preferential selection of green buildings as a matter of corporate policy.

- Use of the growing cadre of LEED Accredited Professionals who can provide certainty about the LEED certification process. The new LEED version 2.2 goes a long way toward providing more certainty through an end-of-design-phase review of applicable LEED credits.

- Stronger use of multimedia approaches and other modern sales tools to increase the connection with green building goals and methods by stakeholders and decisionmakers.

This chapter describes seven keys to a marketing strategy, explores the motivations that drive clients who are the target markets for green buildings and addresses some key points in selling green buildings.

THE SEVEN KEYS

In today's environment, a company must be remarkable just to get some attention. How to make a purple cow (something remarkable) out of a pink sow (something ordinary) seems to be the perpetual task of the marketing arm of the developer's company.[1] The seven keys to marketing green buildings are a combination of two familiar principles of marketing:

- the STP formula — segment your market, target key segments and position your company (Figure 5.1)
- the building blocks of competitive strategy — differentiation, low cost, focus and branding

1. Segment your market.

Marketers try to understand and segment markets in order to focus on the most profitable or available segments. Segmentation variables can include demographics, geographics, firmographics and psychographics. The development market is too large and too specialized to try a "one size fits all" approach to marketing. Marketing resources are limited. Hence, segmentation is required to give focus to marketing efforts.

In *demographics*, the focus is on the social and economic characteristics of buyers, such as age, income, race and ethnicity, and income. So far there is little evidence that this approach to segmentation is useful for marketing green buildings. However, one could argue that change agents who may favor green buildings are more likely to live in politically liberal states, so socioeconomic characteristics could be relevant.

Figure 5.1
The STP Method for Marketing Differentiation

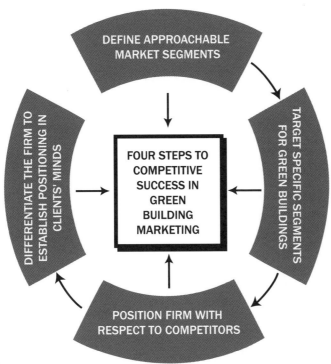

Source: Jerry Yudelson

Geographics — where people are locating and building — is certainly a prime variable to consider in deciding where to market green building services and products. There is plenty of evidence that green building activity is concentrated in the West Coast, mid-Atlantic and northeastern states, with other nodes in the large cities of the South, Southwest and upper Midwest. Comparing the number of LEED project registrations to state population is one way to evaluate the impact of geographic location (Table 5.1).

Firmographics is a newer term coined for business-to-business marketing. The essential distinctions are the size of the company or organization (revenues, number of locations, number of employees, etc.); private, public or nonprofit entity; industry type; and other data similar to demographic data. USGBC data from 2006 show that LEED registrations are clearly more prevalent among public entities (44 percent of the total), institutions (schools, colleges, hospitals, etc.) and nonprofit groups (20 percent), compared with 28 percent of the total project registrations for corporate entities. Project type could also be considered a type of firmographics segmentation and reflects the fact that most clients prefer to hire firms with prior experience in their type of project.

Psychographics refers to segmenting by lifestyle, including propensity for risk-taking and tolerance of ambiguity. In segmenting the market for green buildings, a marketer would look for a risk-taking personality, industry leaders and innovators as early-stage segments in adopting new

Table 5.1
LEED Registrations of Selected States, as of January 2006

State	LEED Registrations	Population (Millions)	Registrations per Million
Oregon	121	3.6	33.6
Washington	162	6.1	26.6
Massachusetts	92	6.4	14.4
Pennsylvania	155	12.4	12.5
California	433	35.5	12.2
Michigan	105	10.1	10.4
Georgia	93	8.7	10.7
Illinois	107	12.7	8.4
New York	164	19.2	8.5
Texas	107	22.1	4.8
Average*	2,805*	280*	10.0*

*Average is based on total of all LEED registrations, not just those listed here.

Source: Jerry Yudelson

technology. Most marketers know who the industry leaders are in given segments and often target them with new ideas such as green buildings, knowing that the vast majority of decision-makers want to see experimentation done successfully using someone else's money before they commit or risk their own.

2. Target specific opportunities for green buildings.

Targeting is the process marketers use after deciding to focus on one or a few segments. It is a critical component in setting marketing strategy because it limits the number of competitive targets in order to focus on those most likely to be successful. Most developers specialize in one or a handful of client types (public, private, nonprofit) and market segments (higher education, warehouses, mixed use, urban offices, historic preservation and adaptive reuse, residential), so the choice of targets is necessarily limited by the company's experience and the project resumes of key individuals. Many developers aim to take greater market share in a given industry or extend the geographic reach of their success in tackling a certain type of client, but most focus on increasing revenues from current relationships to grow their businesses. Developers who have built an early reputation and history of successful projects are often invited to compete for projects far from home, and they are often successful in doing so.

Prime targets for green building marketing share these characteristics:

- They are *early adopters* of new technology.
- They may be *potentially significant users of a new approach* (for example, they control multiple properties).

- They may be *opinion leaders* (and therefore willing and able to sway others, both inside the organization and in a larger community of peers).

- They *can be reached at low cost* (for example, already be clients of a firm or customers for a product).

Since few prospects share all of these characteristics, marketers must choose a target based on a consideration of each of these factors along with some intangibles, which might include existing relationships, stakeholder activity pushing the prospect to choose green buildings, and market forces pushing local entities to keep up with innovative companies.

3. Position your company as a green building developer.

Positioning is the third activity of the STP approach. It takes segmentation and targeting choices and turns them into messages that go out to clients and prospects. One textbook definition of positioning is "the act of designing the company's marketing offering and image so that they occupy a meaningful and distinct competitive position in the target customers' minds."[2] Positioning is a communications activity that aims at changing a target prospect's view of a developer in such a way as to create a difference that makes a difference. These differences should have one or more of the following characteristics:

- *important* in terms of benefit delivered
- *distinctive* — something that not every competitor can claim
- *superior* to other ways to get the same benefit
- *communicable* and somehow visible to prospective clients or buyers
- *preemptive* — not easily copied by competitors
- *affordable* — little price difference to get this superior benefit
- *profitable* to be in this market segment

Developers who position themselves successfully as green building experts by publicizing project successes have found it possible to maintain this positioning even as more companies try to emulate them.[3]

Positioning, then, is what a company does to take real facts and position them in the minds of the targeted prospect; positioning deals with creating perception. In marketing green buildings, positioning is an essential component of a developer's communications strategy and needs to reinforce a single powerful message. Because green buildings are a new industry, they offer the positioning strategy of grabbing a new, unoccupied position that clients and prospects value. For example, a company could claim the most LEED-registered projects in a given industry or location, or the most LEED Accredited Professionals, or the most LEED Gold projects with a certain technology.

4. Differentiate your green development offerings.

Differentiation is an approach to marketing strategy that takes the segmentation, targeting and positioning variables and focuses them on particular markets (Fig. 5.1). This approach, first made popular in the 1980s by Harvard Business School professor Michael Porter,[4] must be coupled with a specific market, geographic or other focus. The main differentiators for developers are successful projects, satisfied clients and tenants, high levels of LEED attainment and the ability to deliver green building projects on conventional budgets. A developer usually needs to show high levels of attainment on at least some of these key variables to develop major new projects in highly competitive situations.

In their book *The Discipline of Market Leaders: Choose Your Customers, Narrow Your Focus, Dominate Your Market,* Michael Treacy and Fred Wiersema point out that every company needs to excel in one of three key areas of differentiation: customer intimacy, product differentiation and operational excellence, while providing at least good service in the other two areas:[5]

- Prospective buyers and tenants may expect customer intimacy in the form of established and continuing relationships between them and the developer. Successful developments are seldom one-shot affairs. Rather, continuing relationships among developers, design teams, builders, public officials and buyers yield the most successful projects.

- Companies need to display operational excellence in terms of meeting building program goals, budgets and schedules while achieving specific LEED goals. For developers, this means getting a product to market within specific market-timing windows and meeting cost and quality goals set by the marketplace.

- Companies that have a signature technological approach such as solar power can often attract clients who are willing to try companies that exhibit product leadership in the area of sustainable design. Developers who focus on such projects as brownfield redevelopment, affordable housing and urban infill mixed use can excel in this area.

Suzanne Lowe outlines the top 10 differentiation activities for professional service firms that might also be used by developers, which are in essence service firms with a product that embodies the service:[6]

1. Conduct advertising campaigns to establish or maintain positioning.
2. Add new services that blend into the services of another industry.
3. Implement a relationship management program to strengthen bonds with clients.
4. Merge with another company to strengthen capabilities and reach.
5. Manage a public relations campaign to highlight achievements and reinforce positioning.
6. Extend the company's services via joint ventures, alliances or referral networks.
7. Add new services to the company within the currently served client base.
8. Create a new visual identity. (Yes, this does work!)
9. Hire specialized individuals, often with control of key relationships.
10. Improve or evolve the company's current services.

case study

The TBL Approach

British Columbia: Windmill Development Group

Windmill Development Group has initiated two Canadian residential projects. The first is a 10-story building (The Currents) in Ottawa, Ontario, with 43 residential units above a public theater representing a brownfield site restoration (a former dry cleaner). For this project, the team is attempting to generate zero greenhouse gas emissions (GHG) and achieve a LEED Gold certification under the new Canadian LEED version. The main designer is Busby Perkins + Will of Vancouver, British Columbia.

The other project is a more traditional condominium townhome development, The Bridges, in Calgary, Alberta, occupied in the fall of 2005. Key advertised features include "unparalleled indoor air quality... high-efficiency appliances... natural lighting optimization... and projected lower operating costs to residents." In particular, the buildings are expected to reduce energy and water costs by nearly 50 percent compared with a normal code building. The partners have prepared a downloadable eight-page booklet explaining the green features and design approach in an attempt to educate and persuade prospective buyers.

Developers Jonathan and Jeff Westeinde, along with partner Joe van Belleghem of Victoria, British Columbia, have been active in the Canadian Green Building Council and in the development of LEED in Canada. The Westeindes joined forces with van Belleghem in the summer of 2003 following completion and leasing of the latter's successful LEED Gold certified project in Victoria, Vancouver Island Technology Park, which converted an older hospital into a high-tech office building and successfully leased it.

Of his approach, van Belleghem says:

> By utilizing a TBL (triple bottom line) approach we try to put our best foot forward and then expand on that with stakeholders to see if we can find innovative ways to try new green techniques in the building. The key is to be upfront and go out of our way to get involved in a community. In our Calgary project, we put in two affordable housing units as we wanted to demonstrate the importance of integration versus segregation. We ensured the units have the same finishes and design quality. They use 50 percent less energy and 60 percent less water so they will stay affordable as utility prices increase. We worked closely with the city, which purchased the units from us. These units have not affected our marketing of the high-end housing and we're hopeful that the city's leadership will have a positive impact on future affordable housing initiatives.[7]

From a marketing perspective, these two developments are making a clear attempt to differentiate themselves through their green building status, reduced environmental impacts and lower total cost of ownership for residents. These projects are market-rate developments in every other respect, but the hope seems to be that an integrated design process will deliver enough savings on system costs to pay for the extra green features. The projects also respond to the stronger Canadian commitment to reduce GHG emissions as close to zero as possible (through high levels of energy savings and purchases of off-site green power) and to subsidize developers who achieve that goal.

Developers can find one or more approaches on this list that will differentiate their services immediately in the green building industry. Research shows that the leading companies are particularly adept at using differentiation strategies such as advertising, public relations, new visual identities and attracting key people. Improving or evolving the company's services typically takes place over the course of several green building projects.

5. Become the low-cost developer.

Given the tight budgets of many building projects and competitive rent structures in most urban areas, the ability of developers and green technologies to compete on price (with low cost) is a valuable asset. These costs may be based on prior project experience, accurate product knowledge, good research, local or state incentives or a willingness to pay to get the experience.

For example, the ability to be creative with green building value engineering for energy and water savings, along with high levels of indoor air quality, might help an engineering company to create far more valuable green buildings for the same fee as a more conventional company. The ability to specify building-integrated photovoltaic (PV) systems would fall into the same category, whether for an architectural firm or an engineering firm. Knowing the costs and the engineering details for PV systems would help an engineering firm convince owners and architects to move forward with these systems.

Low-cost advantages might be more sustainable than even branding as a way to compete in the marketplace, but most companies do not have the discipline to operate in this fashion. A good example of the competitive advantage of lower cost of operations is the almost unblemished success record of Southwest Airlines. For Southwest, the low prices made possible by lower operating costs have become the primary brand, along with fun. Consider that many of the newer airlines, such as Frontier and AirTran have even lower costs of operations (expressed as cost per seat-mile) than Southwest, by being very focused in their routes, not trying to be all things to all people, but offering simple air transportation to budget-conscious business and leisure travelers.

An example of a developer focused on low cost is Workstage, LLC, which is in the corporate build-to-suit market. Based in Grand Rapids, Michigan, Workstage aims to wring out costs from doing green buildings by standardizing every element of the design and construction process. They use interchangeable modules (a kit of parts) and like-minded architect-engineer teams for each project. Workstage's corporate and institutional clients want green buildings, but they do not want to spend an extra penny to get this benefit.

6. Narrow your focus to particular target markets.

The essence of marketing wisdom is knowing which markets to compete in and which to shun, which clients a company wants and which it does not. Sometimes a developer will try to serve too many clients while not satisfying the clients it really wants by being too unfocused. To derive an effective strategy, marketers should consider combining focus with either low cost or differentiation. Points of focused differentiation can include:

- *Regional versus national focus.* Developers may compete nationally by narrowing their focus to one target market, such as mixed use, offices, housing and the like; green building providers may certainly compete with a residential versus commercial focus, or local versus national. Some focus on large projects, while others specialize in projects with a smaller scope.

- *Client types*, which can include smaller clients, psychographic profiles or those distinguished by strong cultures and values of sustainability. Developers and architects who focus on winning design competitions, for example, clearly seek out adventurous decisionmakers for projects that embody a community's or an institution's highest aspirations.

- *Building or project types* (or vertical markets) such as office buildings, public service facilities, higher education, health care, labs, cultural centers, retail, hospitality or industrial. Those building types likely to be affected in the future by higher peak-period electricity rates (up to $0.20 to $0.30 per kilowatt-hour in some of the larger metropolitan areas in the eastern United States), including office buildings and institutional buildings (colleges, public agencies), might be good candidates for energy-efficiency investments, particularly in states or utility service areas with significant incentives.[8]

- *Signature green measures*, such as photovoltaics or green roofs, that a developer commits to bring into play on each project. While it can be risky for developers and designers to always bring certain technologies to their projects, it is riskier not to be known for anything in particular. Branding a company in the green building arena with specific technology solutions for particular building types and sizes can be an effective marketing measure, allowing such companies to at least make the short list for interviews.

- *Project size* can also be a focus, allowing smaller developers, for example, to compete with larger and more capable competitors. An example might be a focus on operations facilities for public agencies.

7. Build a brand image.

In today's commercial world, a major task is to create a brand that incorporates the key differences in a company's approach that make a difference in the mind of a buyer. A developer might want to be thought of as the leading-edge company or product category in order to limit its market but sharply define it to buyers who value that attribute.

What makes a brand in the green building marketplace?

- A brand is a story told between marketer and consumer, between developer and tenant or buyer. The story must resonate with the consumer to be effective. The storytelling focuses on the features of the project and the benefits to the user.

- A brand sells an experience or a series of benefits to the consumer. People must be led from understanding the value of the features to understanding how they will benefit from them.

- A brand delivers on its promises. For example, in the author's own residence, a green apartment building in Portland, the presence of a trash room down the hall, with recycling bins on every floor, reinforces daily the promise that the green building experience will be something different.

- A brand walks the talk. Consumers expect sellers to live by the values of what they are selling. A green developer should have offices in a green building. A green developer should be promoting sustainability in all its activities, not just in a particular project.

- A brand communicates its differences effectively. By some estimates, the average adult is bombarded with up to 2,000 commercial messages daily. Getting through this fog with effective communications is a great art. Most savvy developers hire strong public relations firms and engage in a continuing dialogue with the marketplace as an integral part of their marketing effort.

Of course, we can create differences for each market segment that we choose to address, since some might value innovation, while others value low cost or specific technological choices, such as photovoltaics or roof gardens. Almost without exception, there are very few consumer brands in the green building marketplace today. Without a leading brand (and with due apologies to the major companies involved in this business), the average consumer will not want to make a purchase. Even in commercial situations, the lack of a brand can have drawbacks (for example, imagine the confusion in the commercial air conditioning market without major brands such as Carrier, Trane and York). While a developer can sell GE or Whirlpool appliances to residential buyers, the lack of name recognition for most green technologies forces the developer to become the brand.

MARKETING AS AN EVOLVING STRATEGY

Practitioners need to understand how their marketing must evolve in order to compete effectively:

- They must choose a strategy that incorporates *high levels of differentiation or lower overall costs*, with explicit focus on particular market segments that might include geographic, project type, owner type, psychographic profile, project size, specific technological approach or signature green measures.

- This strategy must be *reinforced internally and externally* so that it becomes recognizable as a brand identity. Internal reinforcement includes training and certification of employees as LEED Accredited Professionals, for example; external reinforcement includes activities to increase the visibility of the firm and its key professionals.

- Larger development companies should consider developing their own *proprietary tools* for measuring sustainability, as part of a branding approach. Along with these tools, firms should develop methods to successfully execute LEED projects without additional design fees.

- Developers must form *close working alliances* with contractors and design professionals to ensure that their green building projects will actually get built within prevailing budget, time, technology options and resource constraints.

UNDERSTANDING DEMAND FOR GREEN BUILDINGS

How should companies think about marketing and selling high-performance buildings and developments? In all cases, the answer comes down to: Who is the buyer? What are their characteristics, motivations, and unmet needs? What elements of green buildings do current and potential buyers value most? What are they really buying? How do various customer segments differ in their priorities? What changes are occurring in these priorities? Do the customers for high-performance green buildings fall into any logical groups based on characteristics, motivations or unmet needs?

Client Characteristics

At this stage of market development, the *private-sector buyer or owner* will be an innovator or early adopter (in diffusion of innovations terms) and somewhat of a risk taker who is willing to balance the strong case for financial and organizational gain against the risk and possibly higher costs of a new approach to building design and construction. Innovators tend to be high-status individuals with higher education levels than later-stage adopters. This type of buyer will respond well to a factual presentation of benefits, will see the longer-term picture, and will likely have done considerable homework before considering the green building approach.

The *institutional or government-sector buyer* is more likely to be an early adopter of new technology driven largely by policy considerations, supplemented with the perspective of a long-term owner-occupier-operator of buildings. The institutional owner is able to look beyond payback to the higher value of such buildings and the positive feedback from the stakeholder base: public officials, employees and the public. These owners typically are more risk-averse than innovators and tend to rely on social networks for information. They want to see solid cost data and preferably local examples of successful projects. They will not be the first to act, but because they are not spending their own money, they are willing to take some risks. The nonprofit sector has an additional motivation: identifying with green buildings has proven effective in raising money for building projects and differentiating organizations in the crowded market for grants and charitable contributions.

Motivations for Green Building

The top triggers to green building among building owners reflect the current focus on reducing energy costs (Table 5.2). How can we translate these triggers into a consistent set of buyer motivations? How do owners, developers, designers and builders see the market benefits of green buildings, and how do these benefits work with the motivations of the various classes of buyers or decisionmakers?

Table 5.2
Green Building Triggers for Building Owners

Key Issue	% of Owners Mentioning
Energy cost increases/utility rebates	74
Achieving superior energy performance	68
Lower life cycle operating costs	64
Have a positive environmental impact	60
Easier to get LEED certification now	54
Secure a competitive advantage	53
Respond to government regulations	53
Secure productivity benefits	53

Source: Green Building Smart Market Report, McGraw-Hill Construction, 2005, available at www.construction.com.

Securing a Direct Financial Return

This motivation can take several forms. For example, a public agency can view financial return in terms of long-term ownership cost, typically using life-cycle cost (LCC) analysis, with 5.0 to 5.5 percent interest rates reflecting today's low cost of public borrowing. A private-sector owner could be attracted by the return on investment (ROI) on energy efficiency investments, using a corporate weighted average cost of capital or some other criterion such as internal rate of return (IRR), employing a corporate "hurdle rate" for discretionary investments. Inside a corporation green buildings have to compete for scarce capital resources, so the financial case for extra investment must be convincing. Other companies use a simpler approach, requiring payback of discretionary investments in relatively short periods of 18 to 36 months. Green building investments for energy efficiency often can provide paybacks of two to four years, with an ROI or IRR exceeding 15 to 25 percent.

Reducing Market Risk

Risk reduction benefits to private developers may increase as more projects achieve a quicker lease-up due to their green certifications. Developers of the Brewery Blocks project in Portland, Oregon, (see Chapter 2) completely leased up their flagship commercial office building, and they sold out the highest-price condominiums in the city nine months ahead of opening. The developers report that energy savings and healthy building features were a factor in the purchase decision for about one-third of the condominium buyers and a determining factor for about 10 percent of buyers. For the office and retail units, the green building characteristics of the development were a deciding factor for some key tenants, such as a large local law firm and the Whole Foods grocery chain, which opened its first Northwest store in the Brewery Blocks.

Enjoying Public Relations Benefits

Many public agencies and large corporations see public relations benefits from green building certifications. For example, responding to a strong public sentiment for environmental responsibility, the city of Seattle mandated in 2001 that all new public buildings larger than 5,000 square feet had to achieve at least a LEED Silver certification. Vancouver, British Columbia, passed a similar ordinance in 2004 requiring LEED Gold status. In Portland, the Earth Advantage program of Portland General Electric provided strong local public relations benefits for more than 60 commercial projects over a seven-year period, through 2003. In New York City, the Four Times Square project by the Durst Organization garnered widespread publicity during the design phase in the late 1990s for its variety of green features and was able to lease up the 48-story office building in 2000 primarily to just two anchor tenants, a large law firm and a major publisher. Another Durst project in New York City, the 2.1-million-square-foot, 52-story Bank of America Tower at One Bryant Park, is aiming for a LEED Platinum rating when it is completed in 2008. This time Durst has been able to enlist Bank of America as a 50 percent partner and 50 percent occupier of the office space.

Improving Risk Profile

Many large corporations and most public agencies are self insured, so it makes sense for them to invest in green building features for risk management purposes. For example, they want to achieve high levels of energy efficiency while exceeding code requirements for ventilation and moisture control. They are also concerned about future large increases in energy prices, especially during peak summer periods. They are meeting these concerns with such measures as lower overall energy use, green building controls, off-peak energy generation from thermal energy storage systems and, in some cases, from on-site generation using combined heat and power (CHP) technologies such as micro-turbines and cogeneration systems.

Securing an Indirect Financial Return

Green buildings increase the prospects of increased productivity, reduced absenteeism and reduced employee turnover, an advantage in a service economy in which people costs often comprise more than 70 percent of an organization's total operating costs. It makes sense to maximize productivity, health and morale with higher-performing buildings, employing such techniques as daylighting, improved lighting levels, greater indoor air quality, operable windows, views to the outdoors, natural ventilation and underfloor air distribution systems. Higher levels of indoor air quality can be marketed to tenants and employees through the LEED certification process or local utility certification programs and through project-specific marketing and communications channels.

case study

Economy, Ecology and Equity

Seattle: Vulcan Development

One of the largest private landowners and real estate developers in Seattle is Vulcan Inc., owned by Microsoft cofounder Paul Allen. Hamilton Hazelhurst is real estate development manager for Vulcan. The company subscribes to a triple bottom line of economy, ecology and equity for its projects. In 2001, Vulcan commissioned the Urban Environmental Institute to produce a *The Resource Guide for Sustainable Development in an Urban Environment* to guide the company's subsequent development efforts. In a recent interview, Hazelhurst said:

> We believe many sustainable strategies will in fact distinguish us in our market and make us more competitive. For instance, we believe strategies that conserve energy and reduce water consumption will be attractive to tenants in a competitive triple-net market (where tenants pay for these costs directly as pass-through expenses), or to landlords in gross markets where operating costs are factored into the base rent and their bottom lines can benefit directly from savings. On the other hand, landlords in a triple-net market who pursue these strategies must be convinced that they will get a rent premium, experience an earlier lease-up or achieve sufficient long-term value for their investment.[9]

Hazelhurst succinctly explains the business case for green buildings for developers with long-term perspectives. Vulcan also expects that their growing reputation as a "good guy" developer will help in future permitting efforts. In addition, they believe that the green building features, including detailed economic analyses of the benefits, will help them in making proposals to large companies looking for space.

Hazelhurst believes that the LEED-CS (Core and Shell) program will help developers such as Vulcan that do not control tenant improvements in their projects. He sees LEED-CS as another incentive to help educate his firm's business clientele:

> Part of what you do as a core and shell operator is to suggest choices to tenants, and it is still a challenge to encourage them to build out their piece in a green manner. But it is a key opportunity to educate end users about green principles, and we're developing guidelines about how they can proceed with that.[10]

In their marketing efforts, Vulcan sells green buildings in three ways:

- Return on investment, in terms of reduced operating costs for energy and water

- Value of productivity improvements and employee satisfaction

- Value-based sustainable features that a company can use to express its commitment to its employees and influence the way in which the company will be perceived[11]

Vulcan has completed two buildings that aimed to become LEED-Silver certified, including a five-story, 113,000-square-foot life sciences laboratory facility, the Seattle Biomedical Research Center, certified under the LEED-CS pilot program, and a 160-unit apartment project. Strategies include water and energy conservation, improved indoor air quality, rainwater retention and reuse on site, reflective roofing materials, low-VOC interior finishes and efficient building systems expected to reduce energy use by 20 to 30 percent.

A new project set to open in 2006, 2200 Westlake, is a 360,000-square-foot mixed-use project just north of Seattle's downtown area with a hotel, 60,000 square feet of retail and 260 condominium housing units. The project plans increased daylighting (a must in Seattle's cloudy climate), operable windows, green roofs, rainwater reuse, low energy and water consumption and environmentally sensitive building materials. As a commercial developer, Vulcan wants 60 to 70 percent lease commitments before proceeding with construction, and they believe the green features help this process along.

Doing the Right Thing

Many developers are leading the way into high-performance buildings because they feel it is the right thing to do and the wave of the future. They hope to create a market advantage, in effect doing well by doing good. The Hines organization (Houston, Texas), which builds speculative offices for long-term ownership, has expressed its view in many green building forums that a LEED Silver certified building would provide a long-term market advantage in terms of lower costs of ownership and a better story to sell to prospective tenants. The buildings owned and managed by Hines professionals strive to maximize efficiency and minimize energy use in creative and pioneering ways (see Case Studies on CD for a description of Hines' 1180 Peachtree development in Atlanta).

Unmet Needs

The marketing task for building developers and facility professionals is to respond to clients' unmet needs by considering high-performance buildings for their next project. In many cases, however, these needs are not articulated well enough to compete with other priorities. It makes sense to use something like the LEED or Energy Star rating system to evaluate a project design and elevate these concerns to the same level as esthetic or other functional criteria. During the course of design and construction, high-performance measures are often "value engineered" out of the project owing to cost considerations. Many LEED projects have found, for example, that the client's strong requirement to achieve a certain level of LEED certification has forced the design team toward an integrated design approach that places the desired LEED rating at the same level as other budget concerns. As a result, the team looks for cost savings in areas other than energy efficiency, water efficiency or indoor air quality, effectively preserving those investments. Often, early-stage eco-charrettes or visioning sessions can help to articulate key stakeholders' unmet needs.

MARKETING MATERIALS FOR GREEN BUILDINGS

Developers and facility professionals need to sell their choices to others. Often it is necessary to make a convincing case to those who hold the purse strings before embarking on the design and construction of a high-performance building. But as most salespeople know, they have to keep selling even after a contract is signed, or run the risk of buyer's remorse after the initial sale. So telling the "green story" is a continuous need.

Developers in the world of commercial real estate use the services of real estate brokers, whose main task is to facilitate transactions for their clients. Brokers need to be equipped with an understanding of the green features of the project, why they are important and what benefits they create, so that they will be able to present them to prospective clients or tenants. Brokers specialize in sales and communications, so considerable thought has to be given to integrating the green features into the marketing and sales materials for the building, especially if the developer is trying to recapture some of the investment in energy efficiency with higher rents, for example. Since brokers are not going to become specialists in green buildings, these marketing materials have to be straightforward and readily understandable by those without technical training.

The best approach is to make the literature about the features of green buildings fit in with the marketing literature for the project. In some ways, this is uncharted territory, especially in the commercial building world. Nonetheless, the basic lesson of sales remains: "Sell the sizzle, not the steak." For technical features of green buildings, this means spelling out and selling the benefits rather than the features. For example, if a project is saving 40 percent more energy than a commercial building, then the pitch to a CEO or COO is that it is 40 percent cheaper to operate, has a high return on incremental investment and offers some protection against future uncertainties in energy prices. If the buyer is a tenant, then the healthier indoor air quality or daylighting needs to be marketed in terms of reduced absenteeism due to illness or discomfort with the space; if the tenant pays the energy bills, then part of the sale is the reduced total operating cost. Convincing a tenant is a harder sell — the promoter risks that the tenant will not value the benefit appropriately, so some form of certification is helpful.

Then marketers need to use all available sales tools:
- a project or building Web site with full explanations of the green features and benefits
- e-mail newsletters or e-zines about the building features, along with links to other sites
- streaming video testimonials from the designers and builders (or current tenants)
- links to favorable newspaper and magazine articles about the project
- attractive signage and explanations in the project's sales office
- radio and TV coverage.

ENSURING SATISFACTION POST-SALE

In the institutional setting, the facility manager and design professionals often share the responsibility for occupant satisfaction. Many stakeholders in a high-performance building (from top executives down to the file clerk) need to know what they are getting in their new building, how it works, what the expected benefits are to them and to their organization and, in some cases, how to make it work.

Without a strong pre- and post-occupancy sales effort, it is entirely possible that the benefits of the building will go unrealized and unappreciated or under-appreciated. For example, in a building with operable windows, who will actually operate the windows? In humid climates, how will people learn when they are allowed to open the windows? When people work side by side, disagreements happen. Research suggests that people will often tolerate greater temperature swings from "normal" if they have the ability to control the environment. In the case of natural ventilation, employees need to be prepared to dress cooler in the summer and warmer in the winter. In one LEED Gold project in Portland, Oregon, the Jean Vollum Natural Capital Center, the building owner (an environmental nonprofit organization) included a lease provision that the allowable temperature range for the building was 68 to 76 degrees, putting tenants on notice to dress for the season.

ENDNOTES

1. See Seth Godin, *Purple Cow: Transform Your Business by Being Remarkable* (Dobbs Ferry, N.Y.: Do You Zoom, 2003), E-book available at Amazon.com.

2. Philip Kotler, *Marketing Management*, 9th ed. New York: Prentice-Hall (1998), p. 295.

3. "New Tricks for Old Dogs," *Building Design & Construction,* December 2005, p. 48.

4. Michael Porter, *Competitive Strategy* (New York: Free Press, 1980).

5. Michael Treacy and Fred Wiersema, *The Discipline of Market Leaders* (Reading, Mass.: Addison-Wesley, 1995).

6. Suzanne C. Lowe, *Marketplace Masters: How Professional Service Firms Compete to Win* (New York: Greenwood, 2004).

7. Quoted in www.betterbricks.com, accessed Oct. 3, 2005.

8. In Oregon, for example, the state's Business Energy Tax Credit, worth 25 percent of the initial cost of PV and/or energy-efficiency investments, can be passed through from an institution or government agency to a for-profit tax-paying entity, on a dollar for dollar basis, making it available for all projects in the state.

9. Interview with Hazelhurst, www.betterbricks.com, June 2004.

10. *Daily Journal of Commerce,* Portland, Sept. 24, 2004, available at www.djc-or.com.

11. Ibid., and personal communication.

Genzyme Center, Boston, Massachusetts, developed by Lyme Properties, LLC.
Photography by Peter Vanderwarker.

JUSTIFYING THE COST OF GREEN BUILDINGS

Green buildings or sustainable construction projects often involve more expense than conventional construction, especially in soft costs for additional design, analysis, engineering, energy modeling, commissioning and certification to relevant standards such as the LEED program. Value-added professional services, for example — including energy modeling, building commissioning, additional design services and the documentation process — can easily add 0.5 to 1.5 percent to the project's cost. Overall, costs associated with sustainability may exceed 1 percent of construction costs for large buildings and 5 percent of costs for small buildings, depending on the measures employed. Higher levels of sustainable building (for example, LEED Silver or Gold certifications) may involve some additional capital costs, based on case studies of completed buildings in the United States.

A 2003 study by Capital-E Consultants was the first rigorous assessment of the costs and benefits of green buildings.[1] Drawing on cost data from 33 green building projects and financial benefits data from more than 100 buildings nationwide, this report concluded that LEED certifications add an average of 1.84 percent to the construction cost of a project — and about 6.5 percent more for a LEED Platinum project. For Gold-certified office projects, most observers expect a construction cost premium in the range of 2 to 5 percent over the cost of a code building at the same site. Cost premiums also vary for new construction versus renovation, and urban versus suburban locations, among many other factors, including variations in local and state code requirements. In the past three years, however, increasing evidence suggests that green cost premiums are dropping as design and construction teams gain experience with green buildings.

Proponents of green buildings frequently resort to rhetoric ("green is good") when advancing their point of view. Justification of additional costs has traditionally rested on the economic payback or return on investment for energy and water conservation measures. Green building standards such as LEED incorporate requirements beyond energy and water use, including indoor environmental quality, use of recycled materials and sustainable site considerations, so it is increasingly difficult to justify green building investments on the value of utility savings alone. This chapter addresses the challenge of justifying green building costs to clients, first by suggesting approaches to classifying green building value and then by explaining some financial benefits from building green.

RELATIONSHIP BETWEEN COST AND VALUE

A recent developer-driven, build-to-suit project in Portland, Oregon, however, has exposed flaws in the idea that higher levels of performance must always lead to higher capital costs. Construction on the 400,000-square-foot, 16-story, $145 million Center for Health and Healing at Oregon Health and Science University is expected to be complete in early fall 2006. The project is aiming at a LEED Platinum rating. If successful, it would be the largest project in the United States to achieve such a rating. The total bid costs for the mechanical and electrical systems are currently tracking about $3.5 million (about 12 percent) below the initial budget estimates. At the same time, energy and water modeling indicate a 61 percent savings on future energy use and a 56 percent savings in water consumption. In other words, from a performance standpoint, this project promises to deliver champagne on a beer budget.[2] This project demonstrates the benefits of an integrated design process and an experienced developer and design team willing to push the envelope of building design in generating a high-performance building on a conventional building budget. The developer puts the total cost premium at 1 percent.[3]

The more developers engage experienced green design and construction firms, and the more they require their consultants to produce high-performance results, the more likely it is that overall project costs will be about the same as the costs for a conventional project. And the developer will get the marketing benefits of a green project.

Many of the green building measures that might give a building its greatest long-term value — for example, on-site energy production, on-site stormwater management and water recycling, green roofs, daylighting and natural ventilation — often require a higher capital cost. While it is possible to get a LEED-certified (and sometimes LEED Silver) building at no additional cost, as one moves to make a building truly sustainable, cost increments may often accrue. Deciding which costs are going to provide the highest value in a given situation is a primary task of the architect, working in concert with the client, the building owner or developer, and the builder. Some systems, such as on-site energy production, are available from third party vendors.

CLASSIFYING THE VALUE OF GREEN BUILDINGS

Green developers must use the language of business, finance and marketing in order to be effective at project delivery. This language includes such terms as return on investment, future value of buildings, tenant market interest and productivity benefits. However, the noneconomic and intangible languages of business, terms used primarily in marketing, risk management and public relations, need to be emphasized equally. In fact, these benefits are often the driving force for key business decisions to build greener buildings.

Building owners and developers have very different approaches to valuing green buildings than do designers and advocates. These *value propositions* can include measurable and nonmeasurable benefits, both for the building and for the company. Examples of measurable benefits include the life-cycle savings in energy and water consumption from improved building energy performance, as well as an improved market position resulting from building a green building. Nonmeasurable benefits include intangibles such as public relations benefits or the prestige of locating one's business in a certified green building.

Green building developers need two approaches to value propositions to validate the incremental expenses involved in green buildings: those that occur inside the building and those that occur outside the building. Inside-the-building value may be created by increased productivity of workers or increased net operating income (NOI), while outside-the-building value may be created by the enhanced image of a company or institution. Other measures of value include risk management reductions, improved recruitment and retention of key employees and increased value of real estate investments.

The classification scheme in Table 6.1 shows how to understand and use green building value analysis. Many owners and developers value other attributes of green buildings more highly than operating cost savings.

Table 6.1
Understanding the Benefits of Green Buildings

Type and Location of Benefits	Measurable	Nonmeasurable
Inside the Building		
Economic	Energy and water savings	Increase in building value
Noneconomic	Increased employee well-being and productivity	Increase in employee morale
Outside the Building		
Economic	Marketing and sales	Brand identity
Noneconomic	Retention and recruitment	Public relations

MEASURABLE BENEFITS OF GREEN BUILDINGS

Benefits to the Building Owner

These costs are easy to measure and include the usual energy and water savings of well-designed buildings.[4] Other benefits might include higher resale value or financial incentives from the government or local utilities (see Table 6.2).

Benefits Related to Building Occupants

There is a growing body of literature documenting the real and measurable benefits of buildings that have enhanced daylighting, natural ventilation and improved indoor air quality. These benefits are found in such areas of concern as enhanced productivity, reduced absenteeism and illness and improved retail sales. Nearly 200 peer-reviewed studies attest to these benefits, according to Vivian Loftness of Carnegie Mellon University. These studies are presented in the Building Investment Decision Support tool (BIDS) developed by Loftness and her colleagues.[5]

Benefits to the Organization or Building Owner

Green buildings may also yield benefits to the building owner through higher rents, higher occupancy rates, or leases from quality tenants. These immediate benefits might also translate into a higher resale value, since the resale value will typically be a multiple (the cap rate) of the projected annual net cash flow generated by the building. Additional benefits might include sizable tax credits now offered by several states.

Table 6.2
Examples of Measurable Economic Benefits Inside the Building

Type of Benefit/ Building Owner	Energy Savings Investments	Water Savings Investments	Productivity Enhancements	Sales Enhancements
Commercial				
Speculative developer	Justify only with higher rents	Justify only with higher rents	Must add to sales value	Not likely
Owner-occupied	Reduced operating costs	Reduced operating costs	Add daylighting and views outside	Add daylighting to retail
Institutional				
Owned or leased	Reduced operating costs	Reduced operating costs	Reduce number of employees	Not applicable

Reducing Costs for Churn

For long-term owner-operators such as government agencies and large corporations with open-plan offices, green building measures such as underfloor air distribution systems (raised or access floors utilizing displacement ventilation techniques) may reduce costs of churn — the propensity of such organizations to move people's work areas, typically at rates of 20 percent to 30 percent per year. Savings of up to $2,500 per workstation in moves have been reported at various conferences, based on an average workstation area of 200 square feet per person. If the underfloor system adds a net cost of $3 to $5 per square foot to the initial cost of the project, that cost is nearly recovered in two years ($2,500 x 20 percent = $500; 200 square feet x $5 per square foot = $1,000). Meanwhile, the benefits of reduced energy costs and healthier air accrue to the project from the beginning.

case study

Making the Numbers Work

San Francisco: 260 Townsend Street

Swinerton Builders acquired this seven-story building in 2002 and turned it into a LEED for Existing Buildings (LEED-EB) Gold certified project. For its headquarters, Swinerton aimed at direct returns from energy savings, improved productivity and the marketing benefits of building green.[6] In the two years since acquiring and redeveloping the building, Swinerton has signed contracts for $500 million of new LEED projects, five times more than in the preceding period. Energy savings are estimated at $28,535 per year, 30 percent below a conventional building, owing to a state-of-the-art building management system. The estimated green premium for the renovation was $1.13 per square foot (2 percent of project cost). The estimated payback for energy-efficiency investments is about four years. Annual energy consumption is about 15 kwh per square foot, up to 42 percent less than similar-sized buildings monitored nearby.

NONMEASURABLE OR INTANGIBLE BENEFITS OF GREEN BUILDINGS

Benefits to the Building Owner

Most intangible benefits accrue outside of the building operations. A few of these are shown in Table 6.3.

Benefits to Building Occupants

Many employees may benefit from the enhanced prestige of working in a well-known green building, or they may have higher morale owing to the better physical and psychological environment. These benefits have always been the goal of architects, but only recently have there been usable tools for analyzing and simulating such features as daylighting and natural ventilation.

Benefits to the Organization or Building Owner

This consideration reflects many of the primary benefits of green building. While most of these benefits are intangible, they are nonetheless real in the sense that they do have economic or social value.

Brand image. Large corporations are highly concerned with brand image. Recent green building projects by such large consumer products companies as Ford, Honda, Toyota (in southern California), The Gap and many regional and national banks, all show the importance of brand image and the role that green buildings might play in enhancing it, by appealing to a customer base of Cultural Creatives.[7]

Table 6.3
Importance of Typical Intangible Benefits Outside the Building

Type of Building/ Benefit	Public Relations	Public Policy	Marketing and Sales	Company or Organization Brand/Image
Commercial				
Speculative (developer)	Somewhat important	Not applicable	May help with loans or leases	Could be useful for developers
Corporate-owned	Very important	Not applicable	Very important	Very important
Institutional				
Owned	Very important	Crucial	Not applicable	Very important
Leased	Very important	Crucial	Not applicable	Very important

Public relations. Many public agencies have sought to demonstrate their commitment to sustainability through the construction of green buildings, including the U.S. General Services Administration, which owns or operates more than 500 million square feet of buildings. Other public entities with strong green building programs include the states of California and Washington and the cities of Chicago, Portland, San Francisco and Seattle—which alone has committed more than $400 million to LEED Silver-certified new building construction in the past few years—and the city of Vancouver, British Columbia, which has a LEED Gold certification commitment for all public buildings larger than 5,000 square feet.

For private developers, the best aspects of good public relations are the enhanced ability to obtain permits from local governments that are promoting green buildings and to get project financing from development partners who see the value in green buildings as a straight real estate investment. In some cases, large real estate investors such as public pension funds might be policy driven to invest only in green building projects.

Enhanced marketing capability. One local residential remodeling company in Portland, Oregon, built the first LEED-certified building in the state, with a showroom for consumers. In the process, it garnered considerable publicity and gained a reputation as a place to go for certified wood products in cabinets and home remodels.[8] Other firms are moving to demonstrate their own sustainability commitments through their building and facilities management programs.

Market positioning. A developer with a strong commitment to green projects and a growing portfolio of such projects might find an increased credibility in the tenant marketplace and an increased ability to win business from major corporate tenants with a strong commitment to sustainability. This approach can also be used in renovating and re-branding older industrial parks.

In other cases, green building certifications might present a golden opportunity to reposition older office and industrial properties as more upscale or trendy. In some cases, the tech bust has left a large number of vacant urban and suburban office buildings in exactly those places where the Cultural Creatives are more numerous and more influential as real estate consumers. Consider the benefit of certifying properties to LEED for Existing Buildings (LEED-EB) or LEED for Commercial Interiors (LEED-CI) with each remodel or renovation. Consider branding an entire development as green with a photovoltaic (PV) solar energy or wind power production system that would be architecturally iconic and highly visible.

Reduced risk of lawsuits. In today's litigious climate, employers would do well to consider how a documented improvement, according to best practices as exemplified in LEED and related standards, might serve as a defense in a lawsuit that, for example, alleges sick building syndrome as the cause for an employee's illness. How much better a defense would this be than merely citing the building code as the rationale for design of building mechanical and control systems?

In addition, is it possible that, over time, this reduced risk of lawsuits might allow insurance companies to offer lower rates for such buildings? Thus, a risk management approach (intangible benefit) might eventually result in tangible economic benefit.

Employee loyalty and attractiveness to new employees. Many organizations seek to show their commitment to employee health and welfare through their benefit programs. Companies and agencies are now beginning to view green buildings as a tangible and positive statement of this commitment. Employees can also be expected to see such benefits as real, especially when the employer takes care to communicate what it is doing and how the building is better. We can also speculate that the prospect of working in a well-known green building might, at the margin, also be a powerful attractant to high-level professional employees. At a current cost of $30,000 to $150,000 to recruit, hire and train a new high-level employee, this intangible benefit might yield positive benefits far more valuable than the cost of the LEED certification.

Doing the right thing. The green building literature is replete with examples of projects moving ahead because the owners or developers realize it is the right thing to do. Unabashed altruism is still present in the commercial development industry, and organizations that want to stay on the leading edge of change recognize that their building programs reflect on their character. As Winston Churchill said, "We shape our buildings, and afterwards our buildings shape us." With an increasing focus on energy conservation and reducing greenhouse gas emissions, the commercial development industry is not likely to remain immune from local government pressures to reduce the environmental footprint of their projects. Why not get ahead of the curve and reap the benefits of being seen as a leader on sustainable development?

VALUE DECISIONS IN PORTLAND, OREGON

Pacific Northwest green building activity leads the nation. LEED-registered projects in Oregon and Washington by the end of 2005 were about three times what one would expect based on population alone (see Table 5.1, page 54). What makes these green buildings valuable to their owners? Why are some projects willing to pay the extra costs of going green? How can we understand what values are embodied in green buildings?

Indirect economic benefits are certainly discussed widely in green building circles, particularly the higher productivity and improved health and morale of employees, but it is difficult to find projects that have explicitly incorporated those goals into the green building design program, except for the inclusion of daylighting (LEED standard met in 40 percent of the first 100 certified projects) and views of the outdoors (LEED standard met in 71 percent of the first 100 projects) as design elements. Most green building projects are putting considerable effort into adding and improving ventilation and indoor environmental quality (with such measures as low-VOC paints, sealants and carpets), which they expect will result in improved morale and health. However, no projects are actually measuring such results, and most projects are not yet spending a lot of effort to educate tenants about the health benefits of their new building.

Direct noneconomic benefits seem to be the driving force in many of the green building projects finished or under way in metropolitan Portland. For example, the first two LEED-certified buildings in the area — the 15,000-square-foot Viridian Place office building in Lake Oswego[9] and Ecotrust's 70,000-square-foot Jean Vollum Natural Capital Center in Portland — were explicitly aimed at demonstrating the owners' commitments to sustainability and, in the case of Ecotrust, a nonprofit foundation, to garner national publicity to help in future fund-raising efforts.[10] In terms of indirect noneconomic benefits, a good case in point is the Honda Northwest Regional Facility in Gresham, Oregon, a 228,000-square-foot distribution, training and office building and a LEED Gold certified project that is intended to help demonstrate the company's global commitment to sustainability.[11] In 2006, the owners have decided to certify this project to meet the LEED-EB standard for green operations.

This desire for recognition as a sustainability pioneer has motivated Lewis & Clark College's new Howard Center for the Social Sciences, recently LEED-Gold certified, according to Michael Sestric, the campus planner, and project architect Will Dann of Thomas Hacker & Associates (www.thomashacker.com). The college was determined to have the new project LEED-certified at a reasonably high level. A second project, Roberts Hall, a 27,000-square-foot dormitory was certified in 2005 at LEED Silver. Sestric feels that much of the college's prior building projects were very environmentally sound and energy-efficient, but recognized that a LEED certification offered an independent measure of the college's efforts to build sustainably and served as a benchmark for continued improvement. Sustainability is the hottest student issue on many campuses, so this approach also satisfied many stakeholders.

In the commercial arena, the Brewery Blocks project in Portland (see case study in Chapter 2) is moving toward LEED certification of all five major buildings (total of more than 1 million square feet of mixed-use commercial, retail and residential), not only to demonstrate the sustainability commitment of its developer, Gerding/Edlen Development (www.ge-dev.com), but also to compete effectively in attracting tenants in a soft real estate market. Dennis Wilde of Gerding/Edlen, long active in Portland sustainable design circles, has been the guiding hand at the Brewery Blocks toward creating the best possible sustainable design. He was very clear that the green goals of this major project had to be met within a conventional budget. Wilde has also created a tenant-improvement handbook to guide future commercial building tenants toward more sustainable choices.

Gerding/Edlen Development has been active in high-performance and green buildings in Portland since 1997 and has registered more than 25 projects for LEED certification since 2000. The firm certainly qualifies as the most active speculative green developer in the U.S. According to principal Mark Edlen, the company is doing more than $1 billion annually now in new development and has expanded its project reach outside of Portland to include major new residential high-rise projects in Los Angeles that are LEED-registered. Edlen also comments that he leased 1 million square feet during a time when the rest of the Portland area lost 500,000 square feet of leasable space.

In Portland, the prospect of LEED certification appears to be a significant motivator for green design, especially in competition with other local buildings of the same type. For the owners and developers this benefit is primarily noneconomic, one they hope will garner significant public relations exposure and also serve as a physical expression of their long-range commitment to sustainable policies and projects. Will we begin to see more green projects built for explicit economic benefits, or will they continue to be designed and built for primarily noneconomic reasons?

FINANCIAL ANALYSIS OF GREEN BUILDINGS

Do green buildings give financial benefits that can easily be captured? Let's look at the potential costs and benefits of building green and see how they might affect a project's financial viability.

Let's assume that a LEED Silver building will add 2 percent to the upfront building cost of a 200,000-square-foot building, costing $200 per square foot to build, with additional land and other development costs of $50 per square foot.[12] The green construction cost premium might be as high as $800,000, which could consist of energy-saving investments, building commissioning, energy modeling, LEED documentation and other related design costs. Let's also assume that with the green costs, we buy a 30 percent reduction in energy costs, valued annually at $0.60 per square foot.

Case Study Example

1. Building @ $200/sq.ft.	$40,000,000
2. Land @ $50/sq.ft.	$10,000,000
3. Green costs @ 2 percent	$ 800,000
4. Total project cost	$50,800,000 ($254 per square foot)
5. Annual energy savings @ $0.60 per square foot	$ 120,000

Value of Annual Energy Savings[13]

At a cap rate of 8 percent, the annual energy savings are worth $1.5 million ($120,000/.08). In this example, the increased value would be $7.50 per square foot. If energy costs rise faster than the general rate of inflation or the discount rate, the net present value of the increased cash flows (which drop to the bottom line as increased net operating income) would also increase.

Value of Reduced Operating Costs

Building size	200,000 sq. ft.
Energy cost per square foot/year	$2.00
Energy use reduction per year	30 percent
Energy savings per year	$0.60
Annual energy savings	$120,000
Cap rate	8 percent
Increased building value	$1,500,000
Increased value per square foot	$ 7.50 (3 percent)

Reinventing the Standards for Office Energy Use

McKinney, Texas: McKinney Office Building

The McKinney, Texas, office building gained precertification at the LEED-CS Platinum level in 2005, with a project that aims to reduce energy use by 67 percent and water use by 30 percent, compared with a similar, conventional office building.[14] WestWorld Management, a European developer, expects to gain the Platinum rating through a combination of innovative mechanical and electrical systems, rainwater recovery and reuse and sustainable design elements. The 61,000-square-foot, three-story office building opened in March 2006. The design team will develop green tenant guidelines to encourage tenants to incorporate sustainable design. The project includes a 45-kw photovoltaic system and buys energy from a certified green power source.

We have secured an increase in value of $7.50, with an incremental investment of $4.00 per square foot. Considering the value of energy savings alone, we can easily afford to spend up to $7.50 per square foot on green upgrades and still break even on the building value. If there are other benefits — such as better public relations, faster permit review, utility incentives and tax credits — an intelligent business decision would be to build green.

Value of Rent Premium[15]

Anecdotal evidence confirms the idea that green buildings may support a slight rental premium, expedited leasing and marketing advantage. Assuming a rent of $30 per square foot per year and a 5 percent rent premium ($1.50 per square foot), building value increases by 7.4 percent.

Value of Rent Premium

Building size	200,000 sq. ft.
Rent	$30 per sq. ft. per year
Rent premium	5 percent
Rent premium per year	$1.50
Annual rent premium	$300,000
Cap rate	8 percent
Increased building value	$3,750,000
Increased value per square foot	$18.75 (7.4 percent)

Value of Occupancy Premium[16]

Assume an average occupancy of 90 percent, and assume that a LEED-certified building will have an occupancy premium of 2 percent because of the positive effect on employee comfort, health and productivity of daylighting, views of the outdoors, higher indoor air quality and other amenities. Building value would increase by 3 percent.

Value of Occupancy Premium

Building size	200,000 sq. ft.
Occupancy	90 percent
Occupancy premium	2 percent
Rent per year	$30 per sq. ft.
Annual occupancy premium	$120,000
Cap rate	8 percent
Increased building value	$1,500,000
Increased value per square foot	$ 7.50 (3 percent)

Residual Value Premium

What about the potential higher value of a green building upon resale? Obviously, if the building is cheaper to operate, has better occupancy and possibly commands a rent premium, it should be perceived as having a higher overall value. In this case, let's assume an exit cap rate benefit of 25 basis points, or 7.75 percent. The building value has increased by $840,000 (1.6 percent of initial cost) just through the perception of value created by having a certified green building in a sea of similar real estate offerings.

Value of Residual Value Premium

Total costs	$254 per square foot, including green premium
Assumed net rent at 8 percent of cost	$20.32 per sq. ft.
Value at 8 percent cap rate	$254 per sq. ft.
Upfront green cost premium	$4.00
Value plus premium	$258.00 per sq. ft.
Value at 7.75 percent cap rate, plus premium	$262.20 per sq. ft.
Increased building value	$840,000
Increased value per square foot	$4.20 (1.6 percent)

OTHER POTENTIAL FINANCIAL INCENTIVES

The story doesn't end here, in most cases. Here is a list of potential financial incentives for building green-certified properties as a speculative proposition, as a build-to-suit developer and as a corporate or institutional building owner:

- Federal tax credits and deductions under the Energy Policy Act of 2005 (EPACT)

- State tax credits and exemptions in various states (see www.dsireusa.org)

- Utility cash rebates, grants and subsidies (typically based on energy savings and/or use of renewable energy systems)

- Reduced development charges or "impact fees" based on stormwater management and water conservation measures

- Permit assistance, including faster permitting (varies by jurisdiction)

- Increased floor-to-area ratio (FAR) (varies by jurisdiction and can allow for greater project height, volume and total floor area)

- Increased financing from socially responsible investors, such as pension funds and green building REITs

- Ability to secure financing through earlier lease commitments and better tenants by using green building marketing and LEED for Core and Shell (LEED-CS) rating system

ENDNOTES

1.   Gregory Kats et al., *The Costs and Financial Benefits of Green Buildings*, 2003, available at www.cap-e.com/ewebeditpro/items/O59F3303.ppt#1.

2.   A case study of this project is available from the design engineering firm, Interface Engineering, at www.ieice.com. See also Jerry Yudelson and Andy Frichtl: "Platinum on a Budget," *Consulting-Specifying Engineer,* October 2005, p. 64–70; available at www.csemag.com/article/CA6271678.html?text=Platinum.

3.   Personal communication, Dennis Wilde, Gerding/Edlen Development, Portland, Oregon.

4.   See, for example, the 200 case studies documented by Rocky Mountain Institute (www.rmi.org); *Green Developments v.2.0* (CD-ROM); and the U.S. Department of Energy's database of high-performance buildings, www.eere.energy.gov/buildings/highperformance.

5.   See the article on this project at www.aia.org/SiteObjects/files/BIDS_color.pdf.

6.   *Green Value: Green Buildings, Growing Assets—Case Studies* (Victoria, B.C.: Royal Institution of Chartered Surveyors, 2005), p. 42; available at www.rics.org/greenvalue.

7.   Paul H. Ray and Sherry Ruth Anderson, *The Cultural Creatives: How 50 Million People Are Changing the World* (New York: Harmony Books, 2000). "The Cultural Creatives are 50 million Americans who care deeply about ecology and saving the planet, about relationships, peace, social justice, and about authenticity, self actualization, spirituality and self-expression. Surprisingly, they are both inner-directed and socially concerned, they're activists, volunteers and contributors to good causes more than other Americans." See also www.culturalcreatives.org.

8.   Personal communication, Tom Kelly, CEO, Neil Kelly Remodelers, Portland, Oregon.

9.   For Viridian Place, see portland.bizjournals.com/portland/stories/2001/12/10/daily18.html. For Ecotrust, see www.ecotrust.org.

10.   Bettina von Hagen, Erin Kellogg and Eugénie Frerichs, *Rebuilt Green: The Natural Capital Center and the Transformative Power of Building* (Portland, Oreg.: Ecotrust, 2003).

11.   See Jeffrey Reaves, "What It Means to be Green," *Environmental Design & Construction,* accessed 5/9/06 at www.edcmag.com/CDA/Archives/54bb4d6efa697010VgnVCM100000f932a8c0.

12.   See, for example, *Green Office Buildings: A Practical Guide to Development,* ed. A. B. Frej (Washington, D.C.: Urban Land Institute, 2005), pp. 28–29, and Kats, 2003, cited above.

13.   In 2005, 51 percent of building owners expected an increased of 5 percent or more in building value, according to the *Green Building Smart Market Report,* cited earlier.

14.   "Reaching for New Heights," *Green at Work,* September/October 2005, p. 30.

15.   In 2005, 36 percent of building owners surveyed expected rents to rise by 1 percent or more

16.   Also, 46 percent expected the occupancy ratio to rise by 1 percent or more; *Green Building Smart Market Report,* McGraw-Hill Construction, November 2005, available at www.construction.com.

Arizona Department of Environmental Quality, Phoenix, developed by Opus West Corporation.

THE FUTURE OF GREEN BUILDING

GROWING GREEN BUILDING EXPERTISE

With nearly 350 LEED-certified projects and about 2,800 project registrations by the end of 2005, clearly there is a lot more information in the marketplace. In many architecture firms and some engineering firms, 20 to 50 percent of the staff have become LEED Accredited Professionals. In one 130-person California architecture firm, all seven principals are LEED Accredited Professionals, suggesting that this firm sees a potential competitive advantage in pushing each project to become a LEED-registered and eventually a LEED-certified building. The development of professional expertise clearly has been a positive factor driving LEED market growth from 2003 through 2005. Most developers should be able to find design and construction firms in larger metropolitan areas capable of executing their green development plans without paying extra fees for them to come up to speed.

COST INFORMATION

As more projects are certified, it is becoming easier to identify LEED-related and green building-related costs, making it easier to budget for such costs in the next project. It is also becoming cheaper to realize green building goals, especially LEED certification, as more building teams and consultants learn how to achieve these goals within conventional building budgets. A 2004 study by the Los Angeles office of the international cost consulting firm Davis Langdon offered evidence based on 94 vastly different building projects that the most important determinant of project cost is not the level of LEED certification sought, but other more conventional issues such as the building program, type of design and the local construction economy. In this study, the authors concluded that there was no statistically significant evidence that green buildings cost more per square foot than conventional projects, primarily because so many factors influence the cost of any particular type of building.[1] If this finding is true for many projects, there will be more pressure from owners and developers for design and construction teams to aim for high LEED goals, because these buildings are perceived to offer higher value for the money spent.

In a 2003 study for the state of California that examined 33 green building projects certified by USGBC, the average cost of achieving various levels of LEED certification averaged less than 2 percent (Table 7.1).

A federally funded study of the costs of achieving various levels of LEED certification for federal government buildings draws differing conclusions from the Davis Langdon study and supports the findings of the 2003 California study. The study by Steven Winter Associates, released in October 2004, carefully detailed for the U.S. General Services Administration (GSA) two typical projects: a new federal courthouse of 262,000 square feet, with a construction cost of $220 per gross square foot and an office building modification of 307,000 square feet with a construction cost of $130 per gross square foot (Table 7.2). The study showed that the incremental capital costs of LEED projects range from negligible for Certified to 4 percent for Silver level and 8 percent for Gold level. It is worth noting that many $40 million to $60 million projects, if faced with a potential 8 percent cost premium, would start looking at integrated design methods to lower a potential $3 million to $5 million premium for LEED Gold.

Table 7.1
Incremental Capital Costs of 33 LEED-Certified Projects

Level of LEED Certification	Average Green Cost Premium (% of total construction cost)
1. Certified (8 projects)	0.66
2. Silver (18 projects)	2.11
3. Gold (6 projects)	1.82
4. Platinum (1 project)	6.50
Average of 33 Buildings	1.84

Source: Gregory Kats et al., The Costs and Financial Benefits of Green Buildings, 2003, available at www.cap-e.com.

Table 7.2

Incremental Costs of LEED-Certifying Two Prototypical GSA Projects

Level of LEED Certification	Range of Green Cost Premiums	(% of Total Construction Cost)
Building Type	New Courthouse	Office Modernization
1. Certified	-0.4 to 1.0	1.4 to 2.1
2. Silver	-0.0 to 4.4	3.1 to 4.2
3. Gold	1.4 to 8.1	7.8 to 8.2[a]

Source: Steven Winter Associates, GSA LEED Cost Study, 2004, available at www.wbdg.org/media/pdf/gsa_lcs_report.pdf.

[a]The author's note: The construction cost estimates reflect a number of GSA-specific design features and project assumptions; as such, the numbers must be used with caution and may not be directly transferable to other project types or building owners.

Understanding the incremental costs of LEED certification efforts is important, because the single most important determinant of the rate of new product adoption is the relative economic advantage it creates. In the construction world, construction costs are hard, but benefits — including projected energy and water savings, productivity gains, and so forth — are mainly soft. Therefore, executing a cost-benefit analysis for each project is crucially important to convince clients to proceed with sustainable design measures and the LEED certification effort.

SOFT COSTS

Soft costs for design and documentation services were also estimated in the GSA LEED cost study and range from about $0.40 to $0.80 per square foot (0.2 to 0.4 percent) for the courthouse and $0.35 to $0.70 per square foot (0.3 to 0.6 percent) for the office building modernization project. One caution on these costs: they run from $100,000 to $200,000 for the courthouse and the office building modernization and may not be reduced much for smaller projects; therefore, the incremental percentage of total cost may be higher for smaller projects. Some typical soft cost elements and their ranges are shown in Table 7.3. Note that version 2.2 of LEED-NC, introduced in November 2005, may cut documentation costs up to 50 percent, but is unlikely to affect other LEED cost drivers.

EXTERNAL FACTORS

Energy and Climate Issues

Outside forces have led building owners, buyers and developers to become increasingly concerned with long-term operating costs. These forces include the growing realization of the problem of global warming (through greenhouse gas emissions); environmental hazards of mold, chemical allergies and other indoor air quality issues; lawsuits related to building mold and mildew from

Table 7.3
Soft Costs for LEED Projects

Element	Cost Range	Required in LEED?
1. Building commissioning	$0.30 to $0.75 per square foot, $20,000 minimum	Yes
2. Energy modeling	$12,000 to $30,000	Yes
3. LEED documentation[a]	$15,000 to $30,000	Yes
4. Eco-charrettes	$ 7,500 to $30,000	No
5. Natural ventilation modeling	$ 7,500 to $20,000	No
6. Additional commissioning services	$ 3,000 to $15,000	No (an optional point)
7. Daylighting design modeling	$ 3,000 to $10,000	No (some utilities offer this as a free service)

[a]Includes outside LEED consultant and architect/engineer professional services time.
Source: Jerry Yudelson

poor design and construction practices; current oil price escalations; and drought throughout the western United States. In 2004 and 2005, the rapid (and seemingly permanent) escalation in oil prices affected the psychology of consumers, building owners, developers and public officials, who are beginning to realize for the first time in nearly 25 years that energy prices are likely to be much higher for the foreseeable future than in the recent past.[2]

The greenhouse gas issue will be a key factor in driving major reductions in the energy use of buildings, including the incorporation of daylighting and natural ventilation approaches. Over the next three years or so, it will not be unusual to see engineers aiming at 50 percent reductions in buildings' energy use (from current codes). Indicating the seriousness with which the business community views the issue of greenhouse gas emissions and associated global climate change, the Conference Board's environmental expert stated:

> Given the increasing costs of, and uncertainties surrounding, the reliability of traditional energy sources and growing pressures for higher standards of citizenship and contributions to global sustainability, businesses that ignore the debate over climate change do so at their peril.[3]

Social And Cultural Change

More stakeholder groups have become knowledgeable about green buildings, leading them to demand such projects for their schools and campuses, health care institutions, museums, libraries and so on. This grassroots support is especially manifested in public and nonprofit buildings, but it will become increasingly evident as public support for and understanding of the concept of sustainability grow. On college campuses, sustainability is rapidly becoming a galvanizing issue for students and faculty, so that the push for LEED projects in higher education is likely to gain considerable momentum in 2006 and 2007.[4]

Technological Change

Many green building measures, such as underfloor air distribution systems, photovoltaics, rainwater harvesting, on-site waste treatment and green roofs, are becoming mainstream technologies that have a strong track record in design and use. As a result, these measures are gaining a strong, supportive infrastructure of salespeople and suppliers, a better cost history, an understanding of how to bid and install them, and a growing number of advocates among architects and engineers who are learning to design and specify such systems. The construction industry infrastructure is quite mature and highly complex, and green building marketers have been mastering its intricacies to get new green building designs, technologies and products into that marketplace.

Economic Change

Lower interest rates have the effect of encouraging capital investments that yield long-term operating cost savings, because the present value of future savings is larger today than in a higher-interest-rate environment. In addition, the relative lack of investment in energy-supply infrastructure in recent years may have the effect of guaranteeing higher future energy prices. As a result, the payback of capital investments for energy and water conservation, for example, becomes more favorable with each passing year. It is fairly easy to justify a 10-year payback (return of initial investment in annual energy savings) for energy conservation and efficiency investments, at least on rational economic grounds, which could lead buildings to be built 30 to 50 percent more efficient than current codes.

Political and Legal Change

More cities and states are adopting incentive programs for green buildings, including direct financial incentives. These incentives have generated significant private-sector investment in Washington, Oregon, California, New York and British Columbia, to name just a few areas. The Energy Policy Act of 2005 (EPACT) provides new tax credits for systems placed in service in 2006 and 2007. If the cost of oil and gas remains high, it is likely that Congress will extend these incentives beyond calendar year 2007. Regulations for these credits are available and developers and other design professionals should take advantage of them for projects that will be completed by the end of 2007.

Legal changes are also occurring, as liability for poor indoor air quality becomes more of an issue in lawsuits and claims against builders and developers, architects and engineers, contractors and specifiers. LEED and other certification programs offer some risk management or damage control benefits by providing objective standards for best practices and independent review of actual achievements.

Industry Practices

In just about every area of the country and every sector of the marketplace, design contracts (and, more often, CMIGC contracts to builders) are awarded based on qualifications instead of price. Fees are negotiated after a selection is made. It is becoming increasingly difficult for firms to qualify for a short list of finalists for a project without having a strong green building orientation, knowledge of green building products and some successful projects under their belts. Competitive pressures alone are driving more firms toward green building projects, even if they do not really believe in the need for them. It is also leading them to hire younger professionals who are green buildings advocates and a positive influence within their firms.

Certification Programs

LEED is not the only green building certification program that affects green building demand. Many certification programs are developing to handle subsets of the LEED rating system; these programs affect building products, indoor air quality, green tags for carbon dioxide emissions, cool roofs, green roofs and other similar measures. State-level and utility programs also serve the commercial and residential building market. Products will begin to be rated for their impact on energy demand, greenhouse gas emissions, use of Persistent Bio-Accumulative and Toxic (PBT) compounds and similar nonproduct features, all falling under the rubric of life-cycle assessment. Users will increasingly be given evidence of a product's origins and full life-cycle impact. Specification writers will incorporate these product features and environmental characteristics in construction documents. As the importance of green-ness grows, products that stand out will be specified and used more.

FORECASTING THE DEMAND FOR LEED PROJECTS

Where is LEED going in the short term and in the medium term? These are critical questions for companies determining how much and when to invest in retooling their development approach to meet LEED criteria. Based on the success of the LEED program in transforming the marketplace for green products, green buildings and sustainable design and on factors such as energy costs, environmental sensibilities, successful sustainable developments and public concern about global warming, it is easy to see that this movement has legs, and any practical developer must pay attention.

Short-Term Demand

Forecasting short-term demand for LEED projects (Table 7.4) projects about 1,661 new LEED project registrations in 2007, averaging about 95,000 square feet (158 million square feet total, about 6 percent of the total nonresidential building market, or about 24 percent of the total available market for LEED projects, assuming the 25 percent number given above), with about 350 new projects receiving some level of LEED certification in that year. This level of LEED

Table 7.4
Estimated LEED-NC Registrations, Project Size and Certifications, 2004–2007

Year Ending December 31	New LEED Project Registrations	Cumulative LEED Registrations	Cumulative LEED Project Size (in million sq. ft.)	New LEED Project Certifications	Cumulative LEED Certifications
2000	45	45	8.4	1	1
2001	230	275	51	4	5
2002	345	620	80	33	38
2003	457	1,077	141	44	82
2004	715	1,792	217	85	167
2005 (estimated)	1,013	2,805	350	156	323
2006 (estimated)	1,282	4,087	485	225	548
2007 (estimated)	1,661	5,748	643	352	900

Source: Jerry Yudelson

activity would represent a significant part of the building industry activity, and it will certainly have an influence on many other aspects of the industry. From a diffusion of innovations perspective, one can see that the green building movement will have moved to the early majority phase of the total available market, with much of what is now still considered innovative becoming commonplace.

There are some key issues to note in this forecast. For example, the biggest hindrance today in registering and certifying LEED buildings is the perceived (and often real) additional cost, which above all determines the rate of adoption of new technologies. As building owners, developers and design and construction teams become more experienced with LEED buildings and sustainable design measures and technologies, the cost premium will decrease, resulting in perhaps a substantial boost to these estimates.

Long-Term Demand

The long-term forecast (Table 7.5 and Fig. 7.1) is based on diffusion of innovations marketing theory and the first six years of data on LEED-NC project registrations, assuming a potentially available market of 120,000 LEED projects (20 years at 6,000 projects per year). The method used is the well-documented, well-established Fisher-Pry model of technological substitution, which yields the S-shaped curve (for cumulative registrations) predicted by the diffusion of innovations theory. The theory predicts a steady slowing of the rate of growth, but a cumulative total of LEED registrations more than four times the 2005 year-end total by the end of 2010. If the average LEED project is $13 million in 2005 dollars (110,000 square feet at $120 per square foot), then the LEED building market would be $31.7 billion in 2010, encompassing about 265 million square feet of new project area. Materials sales of all types to LEED projects (at 45 percent of total construction cost) would equal $14.3 billion.

Table 7.5
Predicted Year-End Cumulative LEED-NC Project Registrations

Year	Cum. LEED-NC Registrations	Annual LEED-NC Registrations	% Growth of Cumulative LEED Registrations
2002	614	344	127
2003	1061	447	73
2004	1774	713	67
2005	2,805	1,013	58
2006	4,087	1,282	46
2007	5,748	1,661	41
2008	7,820	2,072	36
2009	10,344	2,524	32
2010	12,751	2,407	23

Note: Uses the Fisher-Pry model of technological substitution, with an annual potential market of 6,000 registrations, assuming a 20-year market cycle. J. C. Fisher and R. H. Pry, "A Simple Substitution Model of Technological Change," *Technological Forecasting and Social Change 3* (1971): 75–88.

Source: U.S. Green Building Council (data through 2005) and Jerry Yudelson's projections for 2006–2010.

Figure 7.1
Long-Term Projection of Cumulative LEED-NC Project Registrations

Cumulative LEED Registrations

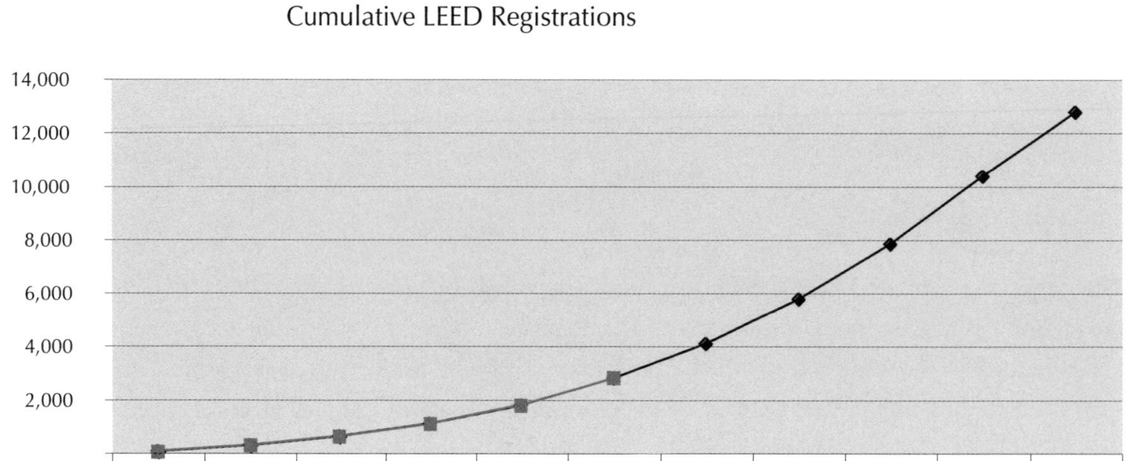

	2000	2001	2002	2003	2004	2005	2006	2007	2008	2009	2010
Predicted Registrations	44	270	614	1,077	1774	2782	4087	5748	7820	10344	12751
Actual Registrations	45	275	620	1077	1792	2805					

Source: U.S. Green Building Council (data through 2005) and Jerry Yudelson's projections for 2006–2010.

Note that the total number of green building projects might be three to five times these amounts, as the number of projects certifying under other guidelines or using the LEED standards but not registering with LEED might be quite significant. These estimates do not consider the growth of LEED for Commercial Interiors (LEED-CI), LEED for Existing Buildings (LEED-EB), LEED for Homes (LEED-H) or other LEED certification tools. These are likely to have their own growth dynamics, based on the economic and social benefits they provide to building owners and developers.

ENDNOTES

1. L. Matthiessen and P. Morris, *Costing Green,* July 2004, available at www.davislangdon.com.

2. In its *Annual Energy Outlook for 2006*, the U.S. Energy Information Administration increased its 2025 price projection for oil by more than 63 percent from the 2005 outlook (www.eia.doe.gov/oiaf/aeo/key.html). In a December 2005 position statement, the American Institute of Architects called for increasing building energy efficiency by 50 percent over 2005 levels by the year 2010 (www.aia.org/siteobjects/files/hpb_position_statements.pdf).

3. www.greenbiz.com/news, Sept. 13, 2004.

4. See, for example, www.aashe.org, a new campus sustainability initiative.

Genzyme Center, Boston, Massachusetts, developed by Lyme Properties, LLC.
Photography by Peter Vanderwarker.

SELECTED RESOURCES

PUBLICATIONS

Building Design & Construction Magazine. 2003 and 2004. Progress Report on Sustainability, ed. R. Cassidy. *Building Design & Construction*, November. www.bdcmag.com.

Building Design & Construction Magazine, 2005, Life-Cycle Assessment and Sustainability, supplement to *Building Design & Construction*, 64 pp., November, www.bdcmag.com.

Gladwell, Malcolm. *The Tipping Point: How Little Things Can Make a Big Difference*. New York: Little, Brown, 2000.

Godin, Seth. *Purple Cow: Transform Your Business by Becoming Remarkable*. Dobbs Ferry, N.Y.: Do You Zoom, 2003.

Kats, Gregory H., et al. 2003. *The Costs and Financial Benefits of Green Buildings: A Report to California's Sustainable Building Task Force*. Sacramento, Calif., 2003.

Kotler, Philip, and Kevin Lane Keller. *Marketing Management*. 12th edition. New York: Prentice Hall, 2006.

Lowe, Suzanne. *Marketplace Masters: How Professional Service Firms Compete to Win*. Westport, Conn.: Praeger, 2004.

Mendler, Sandra F., William Odell and Mary Ann Lazarus. *The HOK Guidebook to Sustainable Design*. 2nd ed. New York: Wiley, 2005.

Moore, Geoffrey A. *Crossing the Chasm: Marketing and Selling High-Tech Products to Mainstream Customers*. Rev. ed. New York: HarperBusiness, 1999.

Porter, Michael E. *Competitive Strategy: Techniques for Analyzing Industries and Competitors*. New York: Free Press, 1998.

Rogers, Everett M. *Diffusion of Innovations*. 5th ed. New York: Free Press, 2003.

ORGANIZATIONS

BioRegional Development Group (www.bioregional.com) is working in the United Kingdom and Portugal on zero-energy developments.

Building industry Web sites include the *American Institute of Architects Committee on the Environment* (www.aia.org/cote–default), the *American Society of Heating, Refrigeration and Air-Conditioning Engineers* (www.ashrae.org) and the *Construction Specifications Institute* (www.csinet. org). See also the annual AIA Committee on the Environment Top Ten awards for a sense of the state of the art in green buildings, www.aiatopten.org/hpb.

Canadian Green Building Council (www.cagbc.org) covers the same territory for Canada as the U.S. Green Building Council does for the United States.

Collaborative for High-Performance Schools (www.chps.net) has published an excellent set of design resources in four manuals for designing green school buildings.

New Buildings Institute (www.newbuildingss.org) publishes the *Benefits Guide: A Design Professional's Guide to High-Performance Office Building Benefits,* aimed at helping architects and engineers talk to their clients about the multiple benefits of sustainable design for smaller office buildings.

Sustainable Buildings Industries Council (www.psic.org) focuses on schools and residential new construction.

U.S. Green Building Council (www.usgbc.org) is the largest (6,000 members) and most significant group in the United States. Publishes the *LEED Reference Guide,* the definitive resources for the LEED system and for green building design in general.

PERIODICALS

Architectural Record (http://archrecord.construction.com) is an excellent source of green building information for the mainstream architectural community and a good way for engineers to keep up with the evolving discussion of sustainability among architects.

Building Design and Construction (www.bdcmag.com), monthly trade magazine.

Buildings (www.buildings.com), monthly trade magazine.

Consulting-Specifying Engineer (www.csemag.com), monthly trade magazine for mechanical and electrical engineering management.

Development Magazine (www.naiop.org/developmentmag), quarterly industrial, office and mixed-use real estate ideas, issues and trends.

Eco-Structure (www.eco-structure.com) is a relatively new monthly magazine that also offers excellent coverage of green projects and materials.

Engineered Systems (www.esmagazine.com) features practical applications for innovative HVACR mechanical systems engineers.

Environmental Building News (www.buildinggreen.com), monthly newsletter. "Making the Case for Green Building," the April 2005 issue, is an especially good resource for a comprehensive statement of the various business arguments for green buildings. Also publishes *GreenSpec,* the most complete guide to specifying green products.

Environmental Design and Construction (www.edcmag.com), monthly trade magazine.

HPAC Magazine (www.hpac.com) covers technical aspects of heating, plumbing and air conditioning.

Metropolis (www.metropolis.com), monthly design magazine that is expanding its coverage of architecture in general and green building issues in particular.

The Sustainable Industries Journal (www.sijournal.com) provides excellent coverage of green building and sustainable business in the Pacific Northwest.

BOOKS

Frej, Anne, ed. *Green Office Buildings: A Practical Guide to Development.* Washington, D.C.: Urban Land Institute, 2005. An excellent guide to broad-scale thinking about green developments.

McDonough, William, and Michael Braungart, *Cradle to Cradle.* New York: North Point Press, 2002. Details the design philosophy of the no-waste approach and issues a manifesto for a new industrial revolution.

McLennan, Jason. *The Philosophy of Sustainable Design.* Kansas City, Mo.: ECOtone Publishing, 2004. Available from www.ecotonedesign.com. A good review of the basis for most of today's sustainable design practice.

U.S. Green Building Council. *LEED-NC Reference Guide.* Versions 2.1 and 2.2. Washington, D.C.: U.S. Green Building Council, 2003 and 2005. Available from www.usgbc.org. A comprehensive guide to the LEED rating system's current version and an excellent contemporary one-volume resource on sustainable design.

Van der Ryn, Sim. *Design for Life: The Architecture of Sim Van der Ryn.* Salt Lake City: Gibbs Smith, 2005. An overview of the present situation and future potential of sustainable design from a master practitioner.

Whitson, B. Alan, and Jerry Yudelson. *365 Important Questions to Ask About Green Buildings.* Portland, Or.: Corporate Realty Design and Management Institute, 2003. Available from www.square-footage.net. Practical questions to ask at each design phase when considering viable green design options.

WEB SITES AND FORUMS

www.aashe.org — At the university and college level, a good Web site is from the Association for the Advancement of Sustainability in Higher Education (AASHE).

www.betterbrick.com — Better Bricks is an excellent resource of energy-efficient and green building design from the Northwest Energy Efficiency Alliance (www.nwalliance.org), a utility-funded organization that offers hundreds of articles, interviews and technical resources for sustainable design.

www.biggreen.org — This Big Green listserv features daily postings.

www.dsireusa.org — State incentives for renewable energy.

www.eere.energy.gov/buildings/highperformance/ — U.S. Department of Energy maintains an excellent Web site for high-performance buildings as part of its Building Technologies program.

www.efficientbuildings.org — covers the 2005 energy tax law's commercial energy efficiency tax deduction. Another site, www.energytaxincentives.org/tiap-gen-info.html, from the Tax Incentives Assistance Project, covers the law more broadly.

www.energystar.gov — U.S. Environmental Protection Agency has a database of about 200 case studies of commercial buildings that have received Energy Star ratings.

www.energytaxincentives.org — Renewable energy incentives in the new federal tax law are analyzed at a number of sites, including the Tax Incentive Assistance Project.

www.esustainableworld.org — Engineers for a Sustainable World is a new group with a focus on eliminating poverty through sustainable development.

www.greenbiz.com — GreenBiz and its USGBC-affiliated Web site, GreenerBuildings (www.greenerbuildings.com), offer excellent industry coverage.

www.igreenbuild.com — iGreenbuild, the voice of sustainable design and construction, is a newer Web site with a variety of content on green buildings and sustainable design.

www.naiop.org/industrylinks/sustaindesign.cfm — Sustainable design and development in industry links section of the National Association of Industrial and Office Properties Web site.

www.poweryourdesign.com — A Web site from New Buildings Institute (www.newbuildings.org) and the source of the Advanced Buildings guidelines and the Benchmark 1.1 tool for designing buildings with energy efficiency and indoor environmental quality.

www.rics.org/greenvalue — the source for the major new U.K.-Canadian-U.S. report on the asset values of green buildings, released in late 2005.

www.wbdg.org — is a good source for the U.S. Environmental Protection Agency's *Whole Building Design Guide* and the 2005 draft *Federal Guide to Green Construction Specs.*

Maryland Department of Transportation Headquarters, Baltimore, developed by Heffner & Weber.

THE GREEN BUILDING MOVEMENT

The green building movement finds its roots in several significant events, including the founding of the Committee on the Environment (COTE) of the American Institute of Architects (AIA) in 1989, the United Nations Rio de Janeiro Earth Summit in 1992 and especially the founding of the U.S. Green Building Council (USGBC) in 1993 (www.usgbc.org).

By the late 1990s, the USGBC had created a pilot program for a new green building rating system called Leadership in Energy and Environmental Design (LEED), essentially a best practices standard across six major components of green building, plus allowances for innovations beyond current standards. This system is now called LEED for New Construction (LEED-NC) and applies to new buildings and major renovations, including high-rise residential projects. The six components are:

- **Sustainable sites:** This category addresses site design, including issues of land use, urban infill, brownfield redevelopment, transportation alternatives, stormwater management, open space, urban heat island effect, and light pollution.

- **Water efficiency:** Considerations include water-efficient landscape irrigation, alternative forms of sewage treatment, and building water conservation.

- **Energy and atmosphere:** This category includes energy efficiency in buildings, basic and advanced commissioning, CFC-refrigerant phaseout, on-site alternative energy production, elimination of HCFC-based refrigerants, monitoring and verification of energy use and purchase of green power from offsite sources.

- **Materials and resources:** Considerations include resource conservation such as building component reuse in renovations, recycling centers in buildings, construction waste recycling, materials reuse (e.g., salvaged brick and timber), use of recycled-content materials, sourcing of local and regional materials, use of agricultural and bio-based materials and use of certified wood products.

- **Indoor environmental quality:** In this category, the concern is for people occupying buildings and includes consideration of effective ventilation, nonsmoking environments, monitoring of fresh air ventilation, construction-period air quality maintenance, use of non-toxic (low-VOC) materials, separation of chemicals from ventilation air, occupant control of building environments, thermal comfort, daylighting and views to the outdoors.

- **Innovations:** Credit is given to new approaches in building design and performance that significantly exceed LEED thresholds or are in categories of environmental concern not currently addressed by LEED.

Altogether, there are 34 categories of credits, with 69 total points. (Figure A.1 shows how LEED credit points are distributed, and Table A.1 shows the LEED certification levels.) A minimum of 26 points is required for basic certification. The LEED system also provides for higher levels of certification, including Silver, Gold, and Platinum. At the end of 2005, 10 projects in the United States had received the Platinum designation, representing about 3 percent of all projects certified.

Figure A.1
Distribution of LEED-NC Credit Points

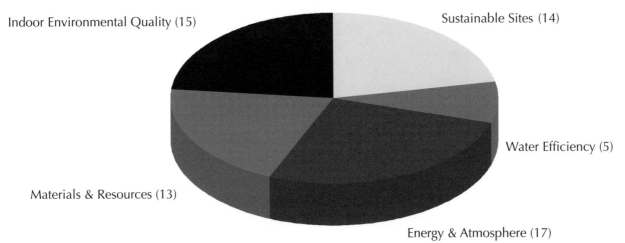

Source: U.S. Green Building Council

Table A.1
LEED-NC Rating System

Credit Category	Points Available
1. Sustainable Sites	14
2. Water Efficiency	5
3. Energy and Atmosphere	17
4. Materials and Resources	13
5. Indoor Environmental Quality	15
6. Innovation and Design Process	5

Certification Levels	Points
1. Certified	26-32
2. Silver	33-38
3. Gold	39-51
4. Platinum	52+

Source: U.S. Green Building Council

The LEED-NC rating system addresses only the top-performing 25 percent of all new and renovated buildings, and it is modified regularly as codes change and as practices that were difficult to achieve in 2000 become more commonplace, such as recycling of 50 percent or more of construction and demolition waste. LEED-NC is currently in version 2.2, and a revised version 3.0 of the standard is expected to be released for beta testing in 2007 or 2008.

Another rating system — LEED for Core and Shell (LEED-CS) — is used in speculative commercial developments to precertify designs to use the green building designation to facilitate marketing, leasing and financing. Similarly, the LEED for Commercial Interiors (LEED-CI) rating system for tenant improvements can be used alone or combined with a LEED-CS project to provide for green remodeling. Finally, the USGBC is developing two new rating systems — LEED for Neighborhood Development (LEED-ND) and LEED for Homes (LEED-H) — for larger mixed-use projects and for low-rise multifamily and single-family residential developments.

Calamos Investments Headquarters, Naperville, Illinois, developed by Calamos Real Estate LLC.

DEVELOPING WITH OTHER LEED RATING SYSTEMS

This appendix contains information about LEED rating systems other than LEED-NC: LEED for Core and Shell (LEED-CS), LEED for Neighborhood Development (LEED-ND) and LEED for Homes (LEED-H).

LEED FOR CORE AND SHELL (LEED-CS)

The LEED-CS rating system expects to launch Version 2.0 in June 2006. LEED-CS follows closely the points and models of LEED-NC v.2.2, for identical credits. The LEED-CS system has 56 core points (LEED-NC has 64), with 22 required for basic certification (Table B1). This rating system allows developers to precertify their projects, attract tenants and financing and then complete the project.[1] One main eligibility requirement is that developers control less than 50 percent of the build-out if they plan to occupy part of a building, or, if they are

Figure B.1
LEED-CS Categories: Point Distribution

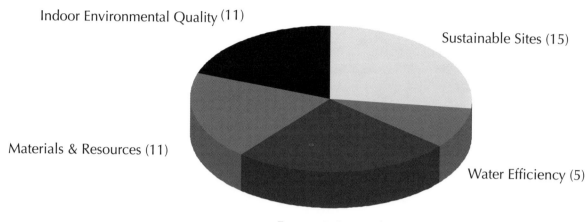

Indoor Environmental Quality (11)

Sustainable Sites (15)

Materials & Resources (11)

Water Efficiency (5)

Energy & Atmosphere (14)

Source: U.S. Green Building Council

not going to occupy the premises, they do not control any of the tenant fit-out. This approach allows a developer to lease up to half a building to an anchor tenant and then lease the rest of the space to anyone else.

In assessing this potential market, USGBC became aware that the criteria and desired timing of certification for the potential LEED-CS developer was significantly different than that for the typical LEED-NC applicant. Most of the buildings that qualify for consideration under LEED-CS are often built speculatively, without a specific tenant commitment for all spaces. For developers to gain market advantage from their LEED initiatives, they need to use their LEED-CS designation to assist their marketing differentiation. For this reason, LEED-CS provides for a precertification of the development prior to construction.

LEED-CS precertification allows a developer to say, "I intend to complete the building with these features and at this level of performance," and the USGBC to say, "If you build the building that you have proposed and document the measures taken, you will be granted a LEED-CS certification at this level." With this distinction, USGBC expects that the developer can more successfully market high-performance sustainable design with a higher level of credibility.

Table B.1
LEED-CS Rating System

Credit Category	Points Available
1. Sustainable Sites	15
2. Water Efficiency	5
3. Energy and Atmosphere	16
4. Materials and Resources	11
5. Indoor Environmental Quality	13
6. Innovation and Design Process	5
Total Points	65

Certification Levels	Points
1. Certified	24-29
2. Silver	30-35
3. Gold	36-47
4. Platinum	48+

Source: U.S. Green Building Council

As one example, the first LEED-CS building in Illinois to be precertified is One South Dearborn, a 40-story, 820,000-square-foot office tower, developed by the Chicago office of Hines development and constructed by Turner Construction. Scheduled for completion in January of 2007, its green features include irrigating large shade trees with the condensate from the building's HVAC systems (a good example of integrated design) and UV-filtration to control bacteria.[2]

Chicago is also home to the first structure to achieve certification as LEED-CS Gold. Developed by the John Buck Company, Inc., the 1.4 million-square-foot, 53-story tower at 111 S. Wacker Drive includes such sustainable features as low-VOC paint throughout the core and shell, CO_2 monitoring, a high-performance curtain wall exterior, extensive daylighting, and a vegetated roof.

Daniel B. Jenkins, principal with John Buck who managed the design and construction, said that "while the green label was a nice draw," it was not a deal-closer. "Most recognize that it's a great benefit, but we did not get more money for it."[3]

He believes, however, that this will not be the case with Buck's next major office development at 155 N. Wacker. The developer, with Goettsch Partners as its lead designer, will seek LEED-CS certification for the planned spec office building.

"Now that we're beginning to market the development, we're finding that anchor tenants are not only interested, but many are demanding space have a LEED certification," says Jenkins. "Many companies now have a corporate mandate."

LEED FOR NEIGHBORHOOD DEVELOPMENT (LEED-ND)

There is considerable interest among urban planners, architects, civil engineers and others for developing a LEED product that addresses larger-scale design issues than just one building at a time. The LEED for Neighborhood Development (LEED-ND) standard is being developed, and it is certainly possible that a pilot LEED-ND certification program will emerge this year. However, we do not think it is likely to affect the development market much until the 2008-2010 period, simply because very few projects involve entire urban districts; most still include just one building, or perhaps the addition of a building to an established corporate, civic or college campus. What may in fact become certified under LEED-ND are cities' efforts to reduce carbon dioxide emissions and energy use, for example, and to improve public transportation options, in the form of new urban plans, zoning code changes, water and waste management plans, on-site energy production with central utility plants and certain infrastructure projects. LEED-ND will particularly emphasize smart growth and green building best practices, including location, transportation linkages, neighborhood design and resource efficiency.

From a developer's perspective, one should look for the emergence of a LEED-ND pilot program in 2006, which will allow early certification of larger-scale developments, probably under less stringent standards than in the final version. This would provide a marketing opportunity for developments likely to occur in phases over several years, as is more the trend in cities, since the costs and timetable for land assembly and development have become so extended.

LEED FOR HOMES (LEED-H)

The LEED-H standard was released as a pilot (beta) test program in mid-2005. There are certainly potential conflicts between efforts by the National Association of Homebuilders (NAHB) Research Center, other local and state organizations focused on residential green buildings, the U.S. Department of Energy and the U.S. Green Building Council to develop a national residential green building standard. Many homebuilders are already responding to opportunities created by local utility green building rating programs as well as those promulgated with increasing frequency by local governments and state builders' associations. The LEED-H standard may be able to meet the market demand for a national green building certification, but it is possible that such efforts will remain fragmented for some time to come.

This new LEED for Homes standard could have a major impact on many mixed-use developments, particularly those with low-rise approaches that are trying to appeal to a new class of homebuyer, the Cultural Creatives, now returning to central cities in large numbers.

About 1.8 million to 1.9 million new privately owned housing units are built annually in the United States.[4] About 1.4 million of those represent single-family detached units, so the market for new LEED registrations is large, assuming LEED could eventually capture 25 percent of the housing market, its stated goal for all market segments. Even 3 percent of this market (the current approximate level of penetration for LEED-NC) would represent 40,000 new homes certified annually, or nearly 100 million square feet (given the average size of a new single-family home at 2,400 square feet). The multifamily residential market may turn out to be a greater adopter of the current LEED version 2.2 standard, because condominium and apartment developers in many parts of the country are looking for the market edge that LEED can create. They also fit reasonably well with the current LEED-NC standard (which can be applied to residential projects above three stories) and do not have to wait for LEED-H to be developed.

Despite the promise of this market at this time, we do not look for a formal LEED for Homes program to emerge from a USGBC pilot test until early 2007. However, this does not mean that there is no interest in green home certifications, but rather that they are likely to emerge under many banners around the country for the foreseeable future. Given that the primary USGBC membership is made up of large corporations, public agencies, design firms and construction professionals serving the commercial and institutional markets, it is not clear that the current membership cares enough about a LEED for Homes standard to push it forward any faster.

LEED-NC VERSION 3.0

Many groups are working within USGBC on the next generation of LEED, version 3.0. Realistically, one would expect it to emerge in 2008, similar to the current version but with more stringent requirements in a variety of sections. Further complications for the next version of LEED may come from the lobbying of various industries either to be included (or not excluded) in the rating system. Therefore, if one can hazard a guess (without having access to any inside information), the following changes are likely to appear in LEED version 3.0. Developers contemplating projects, especially larger mixed-use projects with components that will not begin design until 2007 or 2008, should pay close attention to the evolution of the LEED system, as the certification requirements are likely to change.

- LEED will become more stringent in its requirements to meet its goal of continuing its orientation toward market transformation. This means that, for example, one point for water efficiency is likely to be awarded at the 30 percent savings level versus 20 percent today.

- There will be more focus on absolute levels of energy and water use versus today's relative comparisons. For example, energy use will likely gravitate to the Energy Star system of comparing a building's energy use against all other similar buildings in a region. Similarly, water use will be measured as total gallons per square foot (or kilograms per square meter) of a building, for different building types, compared with percentage reductions against today's code.

- There will be more emphasis on life-cycle assessment (LCA) of materials used in buildings, including the energy and environmental impacts of producing, distributing, using and disposing of them. These LCA tools are under active development and aim to provide a more comprehensive way to choose the materials used in a building.

- LEED 3.0 will likely place even more emphasis on building commissioning, to stress the importance of design-phase commissioning, acceptance testing, performance verification and training of building operators.

- Competing standards for the same credit category are likely to be recognized in the next version of LEED, ranging from certifying green power, to indoor air quality, to a large number of industry-specific product certifications, to requirements for third parties such as Scientific Certification Systems to certify green claims (www.scscertified.com).

- Ventilation and indoor air quality will likely increase in importance. The need for credits that deal more adequately with health, comfort and productivity issues in buildings will increase over the next two years and be incorporated in LEED. There is considerable technological progress being made at this time in new approaches to space conditioning, and the next version of LEED will address these changes with more sophistication and recognition of emerging design practice.

- A number of current innovations, such as 95 percent construction waste recycling, will likely become addressable LEED points as more teams demonstrate their feasibility. This is clearly anticipated by the inclusion of four credit points for innovation included in the current LEED v. 2.2 standard.

Marketers should be positioning themselves to take advantage of future changes in LEED. Those at the leading edge of the green building industry are likely already participating in making the changes in LEED about which we are speculating and will be well positioned to capitalize on them if they do occur. USGBC now allows all members to take part in corresponding committees to stay abreast of proposed changes in the LEED system, so savvy companies should ensure that someone on their staff is monitoring proposed changes.

Developers should be thinking about how to incorporate certain elements of the new wave of sustainable design into current projects, without waiting for them to be incorporated into a new LEED standard. This may be a hard sell to corporate management and lenders who are concerned only with meeting current LEED requirements, unless it is couched in a larger sustainability context and shown to be relevant to stakeholder concerns. An example could be a carbon dioxide emissions mitigation plan (or the purchase of green tags for CO_2 offsets) as part of the energy system planning for a large new building. Finally, companies should be continuing to fund the staff training necessary in all relevant LEED evaluation systems, to ensure that they have qualified people on hand to handle all of the changes likely to occur.

ENDNOTES

1. The Core and Shell rating system states the following about precertification: "Precertification is formal recognition by USGBC given to a LEED-CS candidate project for which the developer/owner has established a goal to develop a LEED-CS building. LEED-CS Precertification is granted to projects after USGBC has reviewed early design stage documentation. This documentation, which reflects a studied and realistic set of project goals and intentions, forms the basis for an award of Precertification at the project's anticipated LEED-CS certification level. Precertification is not a documented and completed building and is not confirmation or a commitment to achieve LEED-CS certification. Precertification is not LEED Certification."

2. *Building Design & Construction* magazine, November 2005, www.BDCnetwork.com.

3. Accessed on May 10, 2006, at www.reedconstructiondata.com/article/CA6316268.html.

4. U.S. Census Bureau estimates for 2006.

index